The Complete Book of Presidential Trivia

The Complete Book of Presidential Trivia

J. Stephen Lang

Fountaindale Public Library
Bolingbrook, IL
(630) 759-2102

PELICAN PUBLISHING COMPANY
Gretna 2017

First edition, September 2001
Second edition, February 2011
Third edition, January 2017

Library of Congress Cataloging-in-Publication Data

Lang, J. Stephen.
  The complete book of presidential trivia / by J. Stephen Lang. —
3rd ed.
       p. cm.
  ISBN 9781455623235 (pbk. : alk. paper) 1. Presidents—United
States—History—Miscellanea. 2. Presidents—United States—
Biography—Miscellanea. I. Title. II. Title: Presidential trivia.

  E176.1.L26 2011
  973.09'9—dc22

                                                              2010048599
ISBN: 9781455623235
E-book ISBN: 9781455623242

Printed in the United States of America

Published by Pelican Publishing Company, Inc.
1000 Burmaster Street, Gretna, Louisiana 70053

Contents

Introduction

One thing for sure about the last few years in America: our presidents have not bored us. The deeds (and misdeeds) of the chief executives have provided endless entertainment. If you think this is a recent phenomenon, think again: all our presidents have been fascinating men. Even the ones who were regarded as stuffy and boring by their contemporaries—John Quincy Adams or Benjamin Harrison, for example—were real "characters" in their private lives. Adams took daily nude swims in the Potomac River (leading to more than one embarrassing incident), Harrison chased his pet billy goat down a D.C. street, and all the other presidents, even the more forgotten ones, qualify as genuinely fascinating human beings.

Whether they were waging wars, quarreling with Congress, romancing their wives (or romancing mistresses), hobnobbing with celebrities, coping with difficult kids, facing off with foreign foes, dealing with death and illness, or just trying to relax, they were always endlessly *interesting*. With people like this in the highest office in the land, it is hard to believe anyone would ever consider history to be boring.

Since these men are interesting, in this book I have tried to avoid dryness at all costs. The arrangement here is topical, with such topics as "Pre- and Extramarital Flings," "Death Sentences: Their Last Words," "Famous Firsts," "Assassinations, and Some Attempts at It," "Presidential Progeny," "Food Fixations," "Jock Presidents," and so on. One can't include *every* subject in the book, of course, but the range is wide—campaigns slogans and slurs, the cabinet, hobbies and pastimes, religion, taxes and other money matters, pets (some of them highly unusual), movies about the presidents, monuments and memorials, burial places, foreign affairs, pre-presidential careers, hobnobbing with the famous and infamous, and many, many others.

The topics are arranged under 11 sections. However, despite the attempt at organization, the book is for browsing. It was made to fill up your time commuting on the train, the hour you spend waiting at the doctor's office, the few minutes before dinner is on the table, the hours on the highway when you and the other people in the carpool are in the mood for a game of "quiz me." In other words, the book is designed to be read randomly, anywhere, and with no preparation of any kind. It is designed to entertain the person who unashamedly likes to be entertained— and challenged.

A brief word about "history vs. legend": throughout this book, I have attempted to indicate instances where a particular "fact" is in doubt. Some "facts" are undoubtedly legend—for example, George Washington and the cherry tree. Some "facts" are very strong possibilities—for example, Thomas Jefferson fathering children by the slave Sally Hemmings. And other "facts" are merely interesting conjectures—for example, that bachelor president James Buchanan might have been homosexual. If there is any doubt about a particular piece of information being true, I have tried to indicate this in the book. Most everything in this book can be vouched for in reputable biographies and historical works. Some of the legends or "might-be-facts" are interesting too, and they are included, but I let the reader know where these occur.

The Complete Book
of Presidential Trivia

✴1✴

Presidential Potpourri

The One and Only . . .

Human beings are incurable list-makers, and we can't resist making lists of "onlys." There's something about uniqueness that fascinates us, and that definitely applies to people as visible as our presidents.

1. Who was the only Catholic president?
2. Who was the only president who did not live in the White House?
3. Who was the only president who never married?
4. And who was the only bachelor president to marry while in office?
5. Who was the only "Yankee Doodle Dandy," born on the Fourth of July?
6. Who was the only president elected more than twice?
7. Who was the only president weighing over 300 pounds?
8. Who was the only one who was elected neither president nor vice president?
9. Who is the only prez whose state of birth is uncertain?
10. Who were the only two sons of presidents to become president?
11. Who was the only president who had served as Speaker of the House?

12. Who are the only two presidents buried in Arlington National Cemetery?

13. Who is the only one born outside the continental U.S.?

14. Who was the only one elected to another nation's Congress?

15. Who was the only president to die in the Capitol?

16. Who is the only president buried in Washington, D.C.?

17. Who was the only president to be married in the White House?

18. Besides the man in question 17, who were the only other presidents to marry while in office?

19. Who was the only president to win a Pulitzer Prize?

20. Who was the only president to have married three women?

21. Who were the only two that died in the White House? (Hint: both military heroes)

22. Who is the only president with a monument depicting him in a wheelchair?

23. Who were the only two who did not attend the inaugurations of their successors? (Hint: They were related.)

The One and Only . . . (answers)

1. John F. Kennedy.
2. George Washington.
3. James Buchanan, "Old Buck."
4. Grover Cleveland, who married the much younger Frances Folsom in 1886. He was also the only president who married in the White House.
5. Calvin Coolidge, born in 1872.
6. Franklin D. Roosevelt, elected a grand total of four times, though he did not live to finish his last term, dying in 1945.
7. The gargantuan William Howard Taft, who weighed in at over 330 pounds.
8. Gerald R. Ford, who filled the slot vacated by Nixon's scandal-plagued vice president Spiro Agnew. Ford became president when Nixon resigned.
9. Andrew Jackson, who was born in a settlement called Waxhaw, somewhere near the state line of North Carolina and South Carolina. Jackson believed he was born in South Carolina, but we aren't 100 percent sure.
10. John Quincy Adams, sixth president, son of John Adams, second president, and George W. Bush, forty-third president, son of George H. W. Bush, forty-first president.
11. James K. Polk.
12. William Howard Taft and John F. Kennedy.
13. Barack Obama, born in Hawaii.
14. John Tyler, that nation being the Confederacy. Tyler was elected in 1861 but died before he ever served.
15. John Quincy Adams, who collapsed on the House floor and died in the Speaker's chamber.
16. Woodrow Wilson, buried in the National Cathedral, as is his second wife.
17. Grover Cleveland, who married Frances Folsom at the White House in 1886.

18. John Tyler, who married his second wife in New York, and Woodrow Wilson, who married his second wife in Washington (but not in the White House).

19. John F. Kennedy, who won in 1957 for *Profiles in Courage*. A number of critics believe the book may have been ghostwritten.

20. Donald Trump.

21. William Henry Harrison and Zachary Taylor.

22. Franklin Roosevelt. The statue in Washington was dedicated in May 1997. There was some long debating about whether the FDR memorial would show him with or without the wheelchair.

23. John Adams, who did not attend the inauguration of Jefferson, and son John Quincy Adams, who did not attend the inauguration of Jackson.

Famous Firsts

What book of trivia would be complete without questions about the firsts? They range from the significant (the first to resign was pretty important, considering the circumstances that led to his resignation) to the supremely trivial (the first to have a middle name). Have fun with these famous firsts, since they give a sort of quickie tour of American history.

1. In August 1974, who became the first president to resign?

2. In the 1980s, what Republican president submitted the first *trillion*-dollar budget to Congress?

3. In September 1960, the first televised presidential debates took place. Who were the debaters?

4. Who was first to see his wife elected to the U.S. Senate?

5. What Massachusetts-born president was the first with a middle name?

6. What 20th-century president was the first to be born in a hospital? (Hint: peanuts)

7. Who was the first vice president to become Acting President, for about eight hours in 1985?

8. Who was the first president born in the twentieth century? (Hint: assassination)

9. During the War of 1812, who became the first president to face enemy gunfire while in office?

10. In 1835 who became the first (and only) president to pay off the national debt?

11. Eisenhower was in charge at the first presidential press conference to be televised. What year?

12. The first presidential baby born in the White House was the daughter of whom?

13. On September 4, 1951, President Truman addressed a peace treaty conference in San Francisco. What was the significance of this address?

14. Who was the first president whose parents survived him?

15. What daring deed did former President George H. W. Bush do on March 25, 1997?

16. Who was the first president to have impeachment proceedings against him introduced in Congress? (Hint: *not* Andrew Johnson)

17. Who was the first to actually leave U.S. soil while in office?

18. Whose was the first presidential funeral broadcast on radio?

19. Who was the first president to wear a beard?

20. Who was the first president to hold regular press conferences?

21. What New Yorker was the first to have a black person as a formal guest at the White House?

22. Who was the first to *walk* the inaugural route from the Capitol to the White House? (Hint: big grin)

23. Who was first to wear long pants instead of knee-breeches?

24. Who was first to be born outside the thirteen original states?

25. Who oversaw the establishment of the first national park? (Hint: It was Yellowstone.)

26. Who was the first to fly the U.S. flag from public buildings? (Hint: Union veteran)

27. What large Republican was first to pay federal income tax on his presidential salary?

28. Who was the first to have "The Star-Spangled Banner" as the national anthem?

29. What Republican was the first to use helicopters for short presidential trips?

30. What Republican was the first president to visit all fifty states?

31. What early president was the first to shake hands instead of bow to his guests?

32. Who was the first to have his wife called "First Lady"? (Hint: wartime)

33. What familiar presidential song was played at a July 1828 ceremony at which John Quincy Adams officiated?

34. Who was the first American president who was born an American?

35. Who was the first to address the legislature of Russia?

36. Who was the first to appear on film?

Famous Firsts (answers)

1. Richard Nixon.
2. Ronald Reagan.
3. Richard Nixon and John F. Kennedy.
4. Bill Clinton. Hillary Clinton was elected as senator from New York in November 2000.
5. John Quincy Adams. (This is fortunate, since it helps distinguish him from his father, President John Adams.)
6. Jimmy Carter.
7. George H. W. Bush, vice president under Reagan.
8. John F. Kennedy, born in 1917.
9. James Madison.
10. Andrew Jackson. (Ah, how times have changed.)
11. 1955.
12. Grover Cleveland. His daughter Esther was born in the White House in 1893.
13. It was the first transcontinental TV broadcast, carried by 94 stations.
14. John F. Kennedy, assassinated at the young age of forty-six.
15. Bush, age 72, parachuted from a plane using a rainbow chute. He was the only president to ever have parachuted, having also done so in 1944 while bailing out of his bullet-ridden plane during World War II.
16. John Tyler, tenth president. The proposal to defeat him was defeated in 1843, so technically he was almost (but not quite) impeached.
17. Woodrow Wilson.
18. William Howard Taft's, in 1930.
19. Abraham Lincoln.
20. Woodrow Wilson.
21. Theodore Roosevelt, who peeved some Southerners when he had educator Booker T. Washington as a White House guest.

22. Jimmy Carter, at his 1977 inauguration.

23. James Madison. (Considering how short Madison was, perhaps the pants he wore to his ankles had been someone else's knee pants.) For the record, though Madison wore long pants, the next president, James Monroe, preferred knee pants.

24. Abraham Lincoln, born in Kentucky.

25. Ulysses S. Grant.

26. Benjamin Harrison.

27. William Howard Taft.

28. Herbert Hoover. It became the national anthem in 1931.

29. Dwight Eisenhower.

30. Richard Nixon.

31. Thomas Jefferson, who thought bowing was a bit too aristocratic, though Washington and Adams rather liked it.

32. Probably Abraham Lincoln. Mary Lincoln was spoken of as "First Lady of the Land," a title which was, thankfully, shortened.

33. "Hail to the Chief," which at the time was probably *not* played to honor the president, but rather played because it was a popular tune. Later, under Tyler and Polk, it became *the* presidential song.

34. Martin Van Buren, born in 1782, and thus the first president who was not a British subject when he was born.

35. Bill Clinton. The Russian legislature is known as the Duma.

36. Grover Cleveland, shown in 1895 signing a bill into law.

Assassinations, and Some Attempts at It

America began with a revolution, but Americans have generally been horrified at assassinations. The usual wisdom is, if you don't like the president, vote him out in four years. But from early on there have been some assassination attempts, with some of them, alas, successful.

1. What alleged assassin was killed by Jack Ruby on November 24, 1963?

2. What federal agency took on the job of guarding the president after William McKinley's assassination in 1901?

3. What Republican president's shooting in 1981 caused the Oscar broadcast to be delayed?

4. Whose assassination was the Warren Commission appointed to investigate in 1964?

5. Chicago mayor Anton Cermak was killed by assassin Guiseppe Zangara in 1933. At what newly elected president was Zangara actually aiming?

6. The year 1881 was a "year of three presidents." Who were they?

7. What popular president of the 1800s was the first to survive an assassination attempt? (Hint: Old Hickory)

8. What Democratic presidential hopeful was fatally shot in 1968 by Sirhan Sirhan?

9. When Abraham Lincoln was shot, which of his cabinet members was also critically wounded?

10. The Dr. Samuel Mudd House can be toured in Waldorf, Maryland. What is Mudd's claim to fame?

11. What former president was shot while campaigning for president in Milwaukee in 1912? (Hint: bear)

12. Buffalo, New York, has a statue of a 20th-century president assassinated there. Who?

13. What president, assassinated in 1881, had said of the presidency, "What is there in this place that a man should ever want to get in it?"

14. Ford's Theatre in D.C. was the scene of what famous assassination?

15. The Sixth Floor is a Dallas, Texas, museum devoted to what famous assassination?

16. What Republican president did "Squeaky" Fromme try to assassinate in 1975?

17. What president was, in 1950, almost fatally shot by Puerto Rican nationalists?

18. The Surratt House in Clinton, Maryland, focuses on the escape of what presidential assassin?

19. What was the fate of Richard Lawrence, caught in his attempt to assassinate Andrew Jackson?

20. Who delivered an hour-long speech after being shot by assassin John Schrank?

21. Who, as a Republican vice president, faced a violent, angry mob when he landed in Caracas, Venezuela?

Assassinations, and Some Attempts at It (answers)

1. Lee Harvey Oswald, arrested for shooting John F. Kennedy.

2. The Secret Service.

3. Ronald Reagan, shot (but not killed) by John Hinckley, Jr. It was appropriate that the Oscar telecast was postponed, since Reagan had been a movie actor.

4. The assassination of John F. Kennedy, shot in November 1963.

5. Franklin Roosevelt.

6. Rutherford Hayes (whose term had ended), James Garfield (newly elected, then assassinated), and Chester Arthur (president after Garfield's assassination).

7. Andrew Jackson. The spunky Jackson turned on his assailant, ready to beat him senseless with his cane.

8. Robert F. Kennedy.

9. William Seward, his Secretary of State, famous for having purchased Alaska for the U.S. Unlike Lincoln, Seward survived.

10. Dr. Mudd treated the broken leg of runaway assassin John Wilkes Booth, quite unaware that Booth had just shot Abraham Lincoln. Mudd was imprisoned for awhile but later pardoned.

11. Teddy Roosevelt, who escaped unhurt.

12. William McKinley, killed in 1901.

13. James Garfield.

14. Abraham Lincoln's, in 1865. The theatre has been restored to its appearance at the time Lincoln was shot.

15. John F. Kennedy's. The fatal shot came from the sixth floor of the Texas School Book Depository, now a museum.

16. Gerald Ford.

17. Harry Truman.

18. John Wilkes Booth, who shot Lincoln. The Surratt family aided Booth in his attempted escape.

19. He was committed to an asylum. The court found him not guilty by reason of insanity. Lawrence, a lunatic, claimed he was the rightful heir to the throne of England, and that Jackson had prevented him from taking the throne.

20. Theodore Roosevelt. This was in 1912, when TR was running on the "Bull Moose" ticket.

21. Richard Nixon.

Naming the Presidents

Sometimes a baby is named just because the name "sounds nice." Some are named to honor someone, say, a family member or someone famous. As you will see from the questions below, some presidents started out in life with one name and gained fame with another.

1. Who was the first president with a middle name?
2. Who had a middle initial but no middle name?
3. Who dropped his first name, John, because it was also his father's name?
4. How many presidents had the same first name as their fathers?
5. Who was originally named Hiram?
6. How many presidents have had their mother's maiden name in their name?
7. Who was named for his father's predecessor as pastor at a New Jersey church?
8. Who was named for the Dr. Abell who delivered him?
9. Who was named for his grandfather, James Knox?
10. Whose middle name was that of his great-grandfather, Speaker of the Massachusetts Assembly?
11. Whose first name was his mother's maiden name?
12. Whose middle name, Abram, was his father's first name? (Hint: assassinated)
13. Who was the only president named for a hero of Greek mythology?
14. Who reversed his middle and first names?
15. Who was named for his maternal grandfather, known as "Honey Fitz"?
16. Who was named for W. C. Linden, a family friend?
17. Who was born Leslie Lynch King but renamed after he was adopted?
18. Who was named for his great-uncle, a Methodist minister? (Hint: He died in office.)
19. Who was named for his maternal grandfather, a Presbyterian minister?
20. Who was named for his great-grandfather, a signer of the Declaration of Independence?

21. How many presidents were named for their grandfathers?
22. Who is the only president to have a president's last name in his own name?
23. What has been the most common first name for presidents?
24. The last names of eight U.S. presidents end in what same three letters?
25. What three presidents went by their middle names?

Naming the Presidents (answers)

1. John Quincy Adams.
2. Harry S. Truman. Both his grandfathers had "S" names, so the middle initial honored both.
3. Calvin Coolidge, born John Calvin Coolidge.
4. *Lots*—specifically, thirteen: John Adams, James Madison, John Quincy Adams, Andrew Jackson, John Tyler, James Buchanan, Rutherford Hayes (surprise!), William McKinley, Theodore Roosevelt, Calvin Coolidge, Dwight Eisenhower, Jimmy Carter, and George W. Bush. Some, certainly not all, were officially "Juniors."
5. Ulysses S. Grant, at first named Hiram Ulysses Grant. When he went to West Point, he found they had mistakenly listed him as Ulysses Simpson Grant. (Simpson was his mother's maiden name.) He went along with the change, not missing the name Hiram. (Who would?) Interestingly, one of his younger brothers was named Simpson.

6. Ten—James Knox Polk, Millard Fillmore, Rutherford Birchard Hayes, Franklin Delano Roosevelt, John Fitzgerald Kennedy, Lyndon Baines Johnson, Richard Milhous Nixon, Ronald Wilson Reagan, and George Herbert Walker Bush (Walker being his mother's maiden name). Ulysses S. Grant is sometimes said to be Ulysses Simpson Grant, but in fact he was born Hiram Ulysses Grant.

7. Grover Cleveland, full name Stephen Grover Cleveland, and named for Reverend Stephen Grover.

8. Chester A. Arthur, named for Chester Abell.

9. James K. Polk. The "K" is for Knox.

10. John Quincy Adams.

11. Millard Fillmore, whose mother was born Phoebe Millard.

12. James A Garfield.

13. Ulysses S. Grant.

14. Dwight David Eisenhower, born David Dwight Eisenhower. He went by Dwight to avoid confusion with his father David.

15. John Fitzgerald Kennedy, named for John Fitzgerald.

16. Lyndon Johnson, whose mother altered the spelling from Linden.

17. Gerald Rudolph Ford, Jr., named for his adoptive father.

18. Warren Gamaliel Harding, named for the Reverend Warren Gamaliel Bancroft.

19. Woodrow Wilson—full name Thomas Woodrow Wilson, named for the Reverend Thomas Woodrow.

20. Benjamin Harrison.

21. Ten—Thomas Jefferson, Martin Van Buren, James Knox Polk, Zachary Taylor, Abraham Lincoln, Ulysses S. Grant (original first name Hiram, after a grandfather), Chester Alan Arthur (his middle name after his grandfather), Woodrow Wilson, John Fitzgerald Kennedy, and George Herbert Walker Bush.

22. William *Jefferson* Clinton.

23. James—as in Madison, Monroe, Polk, Buchanan, Garfield, and Carter, six in all. A close second is John—as in Adams, Quincy Adams, Tyler,

Coolidge (his first name, Calvin being his middle name), and Kennedy.

24. Son. Jefferson, Madison, Jackson, William Henry Harrison, Andrew Johnson, Benjamin Harrison, Wilson, Lyndon Johnson. (And how about Nick-son?)

25. Stephen Grover Cleveland, Thomas Woodrow Wilson, and John Calvin Coolidge. Technically, Grant would qualify, since he was named Hiram Ulysses Grant by his parents, but at West Point became Ulysses S. Grant and stayed that way.

Nicknaming the Presidents

Ah, the joy of nicknames—sometimes admiring, sometimes cruel, sometimes puzzling. A few of the ones below will be quite familiar, and others may leave you wondering "Where'd he get that from?"

1. Who was "Old Hickory"?
2. What early president was known as "His Rotundity"?
3. Why did William Henry Harrison have the nickname "Old Tippecanoe"?
4. Who was "Old Buck"?
5. What 20th-century Republican was "Dutch" in his younger days?
6. Who was the "Red Fox of Kinderhook"?
7. What was Zachary Taylor's "rough" nickname?
8. Who was "Rutherfraud"?
9. What portly man was known as the "Big Lub" in his school days?
10. Who did the vanquished Indians refer to as "Sharp Knife"?
11. What recent president was "Little Pop" or "Poppy" in his younger days?
12. Who was "Young Hickory"?
13. Who was "Tricky Dickie"?

14. Who was "Handsome Frank"?
15. Who was the "Silent" president?
16. Who was the "Rail-Splitter"?
17. Who was "Little Ben"?
18. What philandering Republican was known as "Winnie" in his childhood?
19. Who was known to all his friends as "Bert"?
20. Who was the "Ike" that everyone liked?
21. Who was always known as "Jack" to friends and family?
22. Who was the "Little Magician"?
23. What ex-president became known as "Old Man Eloquent" in the House?
24. Who was the "Great Communicator"?
25. Why was John Tyler "His Accidency"?
26. Who was known by his political enemies as "the Beast of Buffalo"?
27. Who was known, from his Civil War days, as "Unconditional Surrender"?
28. What recent Republican president was called the "Teflon President" because scandals never seemed to stick to him?
29. Who was "Slick Willie"?
30. Who was the "Tennessee Tailor"?
31. What beefy Union veteran was the "Idol of Ohio"?
32. What dapper gent was the "Gentleman Boss" and the "Dude President"?
33. What Southern man was called "Hot" as a boy?
34. What former Ohio canal worker was "Boatman Jim"?
35. What rotund New Englander was the "Duke of Braintree"?
36. What Union veteran was "Wobbly Willie"?
37. What portly man was both "Uncle Jumbo" and "Big Steve"?

38. What wise, multi-talented man was the "Sage of Monticello"?

39. What short Ohio man was the "Human Iceberg"?

40. What Virginian has a place in history as "Father of the Constitution"?

41. Who was "Big Will"?

42. What man was a great military leader but sometimes hissed as a "Useless" president"?

43. Who was "Little Mat" and "Matty"?

44. What short Tennessean was known as "Napoleon of the Stump"?

45. Who was "Rud" as a boy?

46. Who was sometimes called the "Ohio Napoleon" for his habit of putting one hand inside his coat while speaking?

47. What *very* serious Duke University law student (and California resident) got the nickname "Gloomy Gus"?

48. Who was the "Preacher President"?

49. What adopted child was "Junie" (short for "Junior") as a boy? (Hint: Michigan)

50. Who, while serving in the House, was sometimes called "the Madman of Massachusetts" by Southerners?

51. What very laidback man had the habit of dozing off in public places, leading his wife to call him "Sleeping Beauty"?

Nicknaming the Presidents (answers)

1. Andrew Jackson. The frontiersmen knew Jackson as a tough guy, tough as the wood of the hickory tree.

2. John Adams, always a bit chunky.

3. The Battle of Tippecanoe, at which Harrison was victorious, spelled the end of Indian resistance in the region of Indiana.

4. James Buchanan.

5. Ronald Reagan.

6. Martin Van Buren, a redhead, whose home was Kinderhook, New York. The "Fox" name alluded to his political savvy.

7. "Old Rough and Ready." Taylor was known for his plainness and scorn of military "spit and polish." He was a contrast to the pompous General Winfield Scott, known as "Old Fuss and Feathers."

8. Rutherford Hayes. He never lived down the fact that in the election of 1872 there was deep suspicion of voter fraud. Hayes got fewer votes than his opponent, but won the electoral college by one vote—though this was disputed. Hayes was also called "His Fraudulency."

9. The hulking William Howard Taft.

10. Andrew Jackson.

11. George H. W. Bush.

12. James K. Polk, a follower of the principles of "Old Hickory," Andrew Jackson, a Tennessean like himself.

13. Richard Nixon. The name really came into wide use after the Watergate scandal broke.

14. Franklin Pierce, whose good looks were more notable than his political wisdom.

15. Calvin Coolidge, known as "Silent Cal." He was correct when he said, "The Coolidges never slop over."

16. Abraham Lincoln, of course. Like most backwoods men, he knew how to split logs for rail fences.

17. Benjamin Harrison, only 5'6".

18. Warren G. Harding.

19. Herbert Hoover.
20. Dwight Eisenhower. Rumor has it that all the boys in his family were nicknamed Ike.
21. John F. Kennedy.
22. Martin Van Buren.
23. John Quincy Adams, who was both old and eloquent. The name "Old Man Eloquent" was, by the way, taken from poet John Milton's "Sonnet X." This must have pleased Adams, who was a great admirer of Milton.
24. Ronald Reagan.
25. He only became president because William Henry Harrison had died. He became the first vice president to succeed to the presidency.
26. Grover Cleveland, who was from Buffalo and had served as its mayor.
27. Ulysses S. Grant. Note that his initials are "U.S." His nickname came from his demanding unconditional surrender from the Confederates at Fort Donelson in Tennessee.
28. Ronald Reagan.
29. Bill Clinton, who seemed to have as much "Teflon" as Ronald Reagan had, if not more.
30. Andrew Johnson, whose occupation was indeed tailoring.
31. William McKinley.
32. Chester A. Arthur. "Elegant Arthur" was another of his effete nicknames.
33. Jimmy Carter. "Hot" was short for "Hot Shot."
34. James A. Garfield.
35. John Adams. He lived in Braintree, Massachusetts, and was "the Duke" because (his opponents said) he liked to put on airs.
36. William McKinley. His opponents accused him of being indecisive and changeable.
37. Grover Cleveland, whose first name was Stephen.
38. Thomas Jefferson.
39. Benjamin Harrison, who was cuddly and warm with his family, but chilly to everyone else.

40. James Madison.
41. William Howard Taft.
42. Grant. "Useless" was a spoof of the name Ulysses.
43. Martin Van Buren.
44. James K. Polk. "Stump" referring to "stump speaking."
45. Rutherford Hayes.
46. William McKinley.
47. Richard Nixon.
48. James Garfield, who had done some lay preaching for his denomination, the Disciples of Christ.
49. Gerald Ford, who had been renamed Gerald Rudolph Ford, Jr. after his stepfather.
50. John Quincy Adams, whose passion while speaking sometimes led people (especially his enemies) to doubt his sanity.
51. Plump (and well-rested) William Howard Taft, who seemed to enjoy sleeping almost as much as he enjoyed eating.

✳ ✳ ✳

Mr. President, Mr. Author

Most of our presidents had to have a way with words—presenting them in public or on paper, preferably both. More than a few tried their hand at the author trade, and along the way they produced, to no one's surprise, an occasional best-seller.

1. Who was credited with writing *Why England Slept* and the Pulitzer-winning *Profiles in Courage*?
2. What Republican's 1988 autobiography was titled *Looking Forward*?
3. What New Englander published his *Autobiography* in 1929, four years before his death?
4. What much-published man wrote (among many others) *Rough Riders, Hunting Trip of a Ranchman,* and *The Winning of the West*?

5. What professor-president wrote *Congressional Government, George Washington,* and the five-volume *History of the American People?*

6. Whose autobiographies are *Where's the Rest of Me?* and *An American Life?*

7. Whose books include *Midas Touch* and *Why We Want You to Be Rich?*

8. What chunky Democrat wrote *Presidential Problems* and *Fishing and Shooting Sketches?*

9. What former general's two volumes of *Personal Memoirs* were written while he was dying from throat cancer?

10. What Southerner's books include *Why Not the Best?, Keeping Faith,* and *Everything to Gain?*

11. Who published a book about his *Administration On the Eve of the Rebellion?*

12. Who published the 1979 book *A Time to Heal?*

13. Whose four-volume diary of the White House years was published in 1910?

14. What word-happy intellectual wrote *Dermot MacMorrogh, or, The Conquest of Ireland,* a long narrative poem?

15. Whose various books include *The Real War, Real Peace,* and *No More Vietnams?*

16. What early president wrote *A View of the Conduct of the Executive in the Foreign Affairs of the United States?*

17. Who was one of the three contributors to that amazing series known as *The Federalist Papers?* (Hint: He was short.)

18. What New Englander wrote *A Defense of the Constitutions of Government of the United States of America?*

19. What popular propaganda author was thought by many people to be the author of the Declaration of Independence, which Thomas Jefferson wrote?

20. What military man wrote *Crusade in Europe, Mandate for Change,* and *At Ease: Stories I Tell to Friends?*

21. What Virginian wrote *Notes on the State of Virginia*?

22. What bespectacled man wrote *Years of Trial and Hope* and *Mr. Citizen*?

23. What Democrat's only book was *The Happy Warrior: Alfred E. Smith*?

24. Whose many, *many* books include *Principles of Mining, Fishing for Fun*, and *An American Epic*? (Hint: the Depression)

25. What Virginian, as a Princeton student, wrote "Poem on the Rising Glory of America"?

26. What early (and pudgy) president was flattered because many people thought he was the author of the popular *Common Sense*?

27. What Texan published *The Vantage Point: Perspectives of the Presidency*?

28. Who wrote *Discourses on Davilia,* comparing the French Revolution to the American?

29. Who wrote *The Challenges to Liberty,* an attack on the expansion of government under Franklin Roosevelt?

30. Who, after being defeated in his first run for the presidency, described his career in *Six Crises*?

31. Who, while a congressman, published *Portrait of the Assassin*, a book about the JFK assassination?

32. Who wrote *The Audacity of Hope*?

Mr. President, Mr. Author (answers)

1. John F. Kennedy. Quite a few historians seem sure that books were not by JFK himself but were ghostwritten. This may be true of some other books "by" the presidents.
2. George H. W. Bush's.
3. Calvin Coolidge. As expected from "Silent Cal," the book is not very revealing.
4. Theodore Roosevelt.
5. Woodrow Wilson.
6. Ronald Reagan's. The title of the first is from a famous line by Reagan in the movie *King's Row.*
7. Donald Trump.
8. Grover Cleveland.
9. Ulysses S. Grant. After his death, the books helped support his survivors.
10. Jimmy Carter.
11. James Buchanan.
12. Gerald Ford. The "healing" was what he felt was needed after the Watergate scandal.
13. James K. Polk.
14. John Quincy Adams. The long poem was his "therapy" after losing to Andrew Jackson in 1828. It concerns England's King Henry II's invasion of Ireland.
15. Richard Nixon.
16. James Monroe.
17. James Madison. The other authors were Alexander Hamilton and John Jay.
18. John Adams.
19. Thomas Paine.
20. Dwight Eisenhower.

21. Thomas Jefferson.
22. Harry S. Truman.
23. Franklin D. Roosevelt.
24. Herbert Hoover.
25. James Madison.
26. John Adams. *Common Sense* was by Thomas Paine.
27. Lyndon Johnson.
28. John Adams. The writings offended Thomas Jefferson, leading to a break in their friendship.
29. FDR's predecessor, Herbert Hoover, who did not think highly of FDR's ways of coping with the Depression. Historians, and people in general, preferred FDR's methods to Hoover's, but Hoover was correct in asserting that FDR did expand the government hugely to cope with the Depression.
30. Richard Nixon. The book was published in 1962.
31. Gerald Ford, who had been a member of the Warren Commission that investigated the assassination and concluded that Lee Harvey Oswald had acted alone.
32. Barack Obama.

✸ ✸ ✸

Holidays, Holy Days, and Other Special Days

Observing special days is as old as humankind itself. We need reminders of events and people that made us who we are. Inevitably, the presidents had some connections with these special days, sometimes even *creating* them.

1. What president's farewell address used to be read aloud in the Senate every year on his birthday?
2. In 1915 President Wilson designated what holiday to fall on the second Sunday in May?
3. What assassinated president's February 12 birthday became a federal holiday in 1892?
4. On what patriotic holiday did John Adams, Thomas Jefferson, and James Monroe die?

5. Presidents' Day combines the birthdays of which two presidents born in February?

6. On what Christian holiday was Abraham Lincoln shot? (Hint: pre-Easter)

7. By a 1966 presidential proclamation, what holiday was fixed as the third Sunday in June?

8. In 1789 what fall holiday became the first U.S. holiday designated by presidential proclamation?

9. What Vermont-born president was a real "Yankee Doodle Dandy," born on the 4th of July?

10. When Andrew Jackson invited all D.C. residents to the White House on Washington's birthday, 1837, what large food item were they served?

Holidays, Holy Days, and Other Special Days (answers)

1. George Washington's.

2. Mother's Day.

3. Abraham Lincoln's.

4. July 4.

5. George Washington (Feb. 22) and Abraham Lincoln (Feb. 12).

6. Good Friday. Lincoln supporters made much of the coincidence that Lincoln, like Christ, had died on Good Friday.

7. Father's Day.

8. Thanksgiving.

9. Calvin Coolidge, born in Plymouth, Vermont, in 1872.

10. A 1,400-pound cheese, a gift to Jackson from admiring New Yorkers. It sat in the White House vestibule for two years until Jackson made it a gift to all D.C. dwellers.

Famous Firsts (Part 2)

1. What handsome, silver-haired Republican was the first president for which women could vote?

2. Who was the first to be photographed while in office? (Hint: Tennessee)

3. Who was the first to refer to his D.C. home as the White House? (Hint: mustache)

4. Who was first to ride in an automobile?

5. What early president was the first victim of an assassination attempt?

6. Who was the first president—and, in fact, the first *American*—to have a Medicare card?

7. Who was the first to serve as a senator?

8. Who was giving a speech during America's first transcontinental TV broadcast in 1951?

9. Who presided over the first televised cabinet meeting?

10. Who was the first who was not born a British subject?

11. Whose was the first presidential face on a U.S. coin? (Hint: copper)

12. Who was the first whose parents were both alive at the time of his inauguration? (Hint: Civil War)

13. Who was the first to appear in a film?

14. Who was first to be sworn into office in Washington?

15. Who was the first to be commonly referred to by his initials?

16. Who was the first to be born west of the Mississippi? (Hint: Quaker)

17. Who was the first to use a campaign photo of himself shirtless?

18. Who was first to have a veto overridden by Congress?

19. Who, in the 1970s, became the first to visit Japan while in office?

20. Who was president at the first inaugural ball held in D.C.?

21. Who was the first president whose death brought no official recognition from the federal government?

22. What 20th-century Republican was the first to have a national budget prepared?

23. Who was first to be president of fifty states?

24. In April 1792, Washington became the first to exercise what presidential power?

25. Who, riding on the B & O in 1833, became the first prez to ride on a train?

26. What famous first occurred when Andrew Jackson appointed Roger Taney as Secretary of the Treasury?

27. What did Franklin Pierce become the first to do in his inaugural address?

28. Who was first to be present at his nominating convention? (Hint: Union veteran)

29. What brassy man was, appropriately, the first to fly in a plane?

30. What 20th-century Democrat was the first president to visit Europe while in office?

31. What Republican's election victory was the first to be broadcast via radio?

32. Who was the first to take the oath of office in the White House?

33. Who was the first president to publish a book about a president?

34. Who was the first to assume office during a major war?

35. What honest Republican was the first Eagle Scout to become president?

36. Who was president when the first baby was born in the White House?

37. Who was first to have his inaugural message sent out by wire?

38. Who was first to have his inauguration photographed?

39. Who was first to have his own valet in the White House?

40. Who was the first for whom "Hail to the Chief" was played whenever he entered a room? (Hint: Tennessean)

Famous Firsts (Part 2) (answers)

1. Warren Harding. The Nineteenth Amendment, giving women the vote, passed shortly before the 1920 election.

2. James K. Polk. There are photographs of earlier presidents such as Jackson and John Quincy Adams, but these were taken *after* those men left office.

3. Theodore Roosevelt. Prior to his term of office, the house had been called either the President's House or the Executive Mansion.

4. Again, Theodore Roosevelt.

5. Andrew Jackson, the seventh president. The gritty Jackson was prepared to beat the man with his cane.
6. Harry S. Truman. He had card Number 1, and his wife Bess had card Number 2.
7. James Monroe of Virginia.
8. Harry Truman, speaking at a conference in San Francisco. The broadcast was carried by 94 stations.
9. Dwight Eisenhower, on October 25, 1954.
10. Martin Van Buren, born in 1782.
11. Abraham Lincoln. The Mint starting making Lincoln pennies in 1909.
12. Ulysses S. Grant. In fact, neither of his parents did attend his inauguration.
13. William McKinley. His friend Thomas Edison made a short film of him.
14. Thomas Jefferson.
15. TR, Theodore Roosevelt.
16. Herbert Hoover, born in Iowa.
17. John F. Kennedy. The photo shows him bare-chested on his navy ship, the PT-109.
18. John Tyler. It happened on his last day in office.
19. Gerald Ford, in 1974.
20. James Madison. It was held in Long's Hotel.
21. John Tyler. He died in 1862, at the time an official of the Confederacy, so the authorities in Washington chose to ignore his passing.
22. Warren Harding, who had Charles G. Dawes as the nation's first budget director.
33. Dwight Eisenhower. Alaska and Hawaii were admitted as states in 1959.
24. The veto.
25. Andrew Jackson.
26. The Senate rejected him—the first time a cabinet appointment had been turned down.
27. He memorized it, using no notes at all.

28. James Garfield, present at the Republican convention of 1880.
29. Theodore Roosevelt. He did this *after* his presidency, not during it.
30. Woodrow Wilson, who went in 1918 after World War I ended to press for his Fourteen Points and the League of Nations.
31. Warren Harding, in November 1920.
32. Rutherford Hayes, who was sworn into office in the Red Room.
33. Herbert Hoover, who published *The Ordeal of Woodrow Wilson.*
34. Harry Truman, who took office in 1945 during World War II. (In case anyone answered "Andrew Johnson" to this question, that answer is *sort of* correct, for the Civil War was not technically over when Lincoln was assassinated. Even so, it was practically finished at the time Johnson took over.)
35. Gerald Ford.
36. Thomas Jefferson, whose grandson James Madison Randolph was born there.
37. James K. Polk. At his inauguration, Samuel Morse, inventor of the telegraph, sat nearby and tapped out the entire inaugural address in code.
38. James Buchanan, in 1857.
39. Chester Arthur, "the Dude."
40. James K. Polk. Supposedly his wife Sarah liked for the song to be played so that people in the room would know that the vertically challenged Polk had entered.

✳   ✳   ✳

The One and Only (Part 2)

1. Who was the only president given the oath of office by his own father? (Hint: Vermont)
2. Who was the only one to serve in the House after his presidency? (Hint: famous dad)
3. Who was the only one who had been a preacher?
4. Who were the only 20th-century presidents to end major wars, as they had promised?

5. Which two were the only ones whose terms ended and began in the same year?

6. Who was the only one to die in the 1700s?

7. What 20th-century Republican was the only ambidextrous president?

8. Who was the only one to have his U.S. citizenship restored to him by a later president?

9. What was the only First Family that shared the same monogram?

10. Who was the only prez to get a speeding ticket in D.C. while in office? (Hint: Civil War)

11. Who was the only elected president who had less than a week between winning the election and being inaugurated?

12. Who was the only one who knew his wife when she was an infant?

13. Who was the only one who was a second-generation American? (Hint: hickory)

14. Who was the only one to grow up speaking Dutch as his first language?

15. What is the distinction of Franklin Pierce's cabinet?

16. What two-term Democrat was the only president who personally had executed a man by hanging?

17. Who was the only one who was *not* an American citizen at the time of his death?

18. Who was the only one to have an *earned* doctoral degree?

19. Who was the only one to run a ferry service across the Potomac?

20. Who was the only one who could write with both hands at the same time? (Hint: assassinated)

21. What Democrat was the only 20th-century president to never have attended college?

22. Who was the only president with a degree from the University of Pennsylvania?

The One and Only (Part 2)(answers)

1. Calvin Coolidge, who was staying at his father's home when President Harding died. As a notary, his father was "official" enough to swear him in.

2. John Quincy Adams, who served many years as a congressman from Massachusetts.

3. James Garfield, 20th president, a Disciples of Christ preacher who once baptized 40 converts during a two-week evangelistic campaign.

4. Dwight Eisenhower (the Korean War) and Richard Nixon (the war in Vietnam).

5. William Henry Harrison (1841) and James Garfield (1881). Both men died in office.

6. George Washington, who died in 1799.

7. Gerald Ford, who is, depending on the occasion, both right- and left-handed.

8. John Tyler, who died in 1862 as a citizen (and congressman) of the Confederate States. More than a century later, his U.S. citizenship was restored during the Carter administration.

9. Lyndon Johnson's—with Lyndon Baines Johnson, Lady Bird Johnson, Lynda Bird Johnson, Luci Baines Johnson, plus a dog named Little Beagle Johnson.

10. Ulysses S. Grant, who at the time was driving a gig, a two-horse

carriage. He was stopped by an M Street cop who (obviously) did not recognize the president.

11. Rutherford Hayes. The disputed election of 1876 led to a congressional commission that did not decide in Hayes's favor till three days before his inauguration in March 1877.

12. Grover Cleveland, who was devoted to Frances Folsom, the daughter of his bosom friend Oscar Folsom—so devoted that he married her when she was twenty-one.

13. Andrew Jackson. Both of his parents were born in Ireland.

14. Martin Van Buren, reared in the mostly Dutch town of Kinderhook, New York.

15. They all stayed throughout his entire term. Pierce was the only president who never made a single change in his cabinet.

16. Grover Cleveland, who as sheriff of Erie County, New York, himself sprang the trap to hang *two* men.

17. John Tyler, who was not only a citizen of the Confederate States of America, but had been elected to its Congress.

18. Woodrow Wilson, with a Ph.D. from Johns Hopkins University, among his many other degrees. (Several presidents, by the way, have had *honorary* doctorates bestowed upon them.)

19. George Washington, in his first year as president. (Recall that this was *before* the U.S. capital was on the Potomac.)

20. James Garfield. Even more remarkably, he could write Greek with one hand and Latin with the other.

21. Harry Truman.

22. Donald Trump, B.S. in economics, 1968.

CHAPTER

✳ 2 ✳

Mixing and Mingling

Pre- and Extramarital Flings

Most of our chief executives have been faithful family men. (In that respect, they come off looking much better than most European monarchs or Third World dictators.) On the other hand, there were also a few non-marital dalliances, both before and after marriage. "To err is human," and some cynics might say, "To philander is presidential."

1. Who was "that woman" that Bill Clinton most emphatically "did not have sexual relations with"?
2. Who was dogged throughout his public life by rumors about his affair with "Dusky Sally"?
3. Whose longtime mistress Lucy Mercer was with him when he died in 1945?
4. Maria Halpin was the mother of whose illegitimate son?
5. What Massachusetts boy supposedly lost his virginity at age seventeen in a Harlem brothel?
6. Who fell madly in love with a French actress when he was fourteen and living in Paris?
7. Who registered in hotels with his "niece," Nan Britton?
8. Who had an intense passion for an English painter's wife named Maria Cosway?

9. Who was rumored to have had a raging passion for Ann Rutledge, daughter of an Illinois tavern-keeper?

10. What former preacher horrified his wife with his affair with a Mrs. Calhoun of New York?

11. What military man had a youthful passion for an unknown "Miss M" of Philadelphia?

12. What president might have been—*maybe*—homosexual?

13. Who was accused while president of trying to seduce Betsy Walker, a neighbor's wife?

14. What early president was, we feel fairly certain, familiar with prostitutes? (Hint: frontiersman)

15. Whose early crushes fell on Sally Fairfax and Betsy Fauntleroy?

16. What military man considered divorcing his wife and marrying his driver, Kay Summersby?

17. What diminutive man had a raging passion for Kitty Floyd, the fifteen-year-old daughter of a fellow congressman?

18. Who had a long-term fling with Carrie Phillips, wife of an old friend?

19. What Texan supposedly had a thirty-year affair with a woman named Alice Glass?

20. Who came close to marrying his high school and college sweetheart, "Mugs" Cleaver?

21. Who had what he called a "torrid four-year love affair" with Phyllis Brown, a fellow fashion model?

22. Who admitted in a *Playboy* interview that he had committed adultery, but only "in his heart"?

23. Who was accused of causing the suicide of his fiancée, who was convinced he only wanted to marry her for money?

24. What Democrat supposedly shared Marilyn Monroe and other mistresses with his brother?

25. Whose mistress became his second wife?

Pre- and Extramarital Flings (answers)

1. An intern named Monica Lewinsky.

2. Thomas Jefferson. "Dusky Sally" was his slave, Sally Hemmings, who (it now seems pretty certain) bore him several children.

3. Franklin Roosevelt. Mercer had been his wife's secretary, and when his wife learned of the affair, she threatened to divorce FDR unless he broke it off. The affair resumed later on, however. When FDR died in Georgia, Lucy was quickly removed before Eleanor arrived.

4. Grover Cleveland's—maybe. Cleveland was one of several men with whom the woman "kept company." Since the other men were married, Cleveland accepted responsibility for supporting the child, even though he wasn't certain it was his. The scandal broke when Cleveland was campaigning for the presidency. He won anyway.

5. John F. Kennedy, according to one source.

6. John Quincy Adams. We don't know her name, only that she appeared in his dreams for years.

7. Warren Harding. She was more than thirty years younger than Harding. She claimed her daughter was his, and after his death published a tell-all book.

8. Thomas Jefferson, while he was U.S. ambassador in Paris. Whether he and the charming Maria ever consummated the affair is not known, but it certainly was intense.

9. Abraham Lincoln. His law partner William Herndon claimed she was the only woman Lincoln ever really loved.

10. James A. Garfield, who was caught in the affair in 1862. He broke off the affair and was forgiven, and he even managed to retrieve from the woman letters he had sent her.

11. William Henry Harrison.

12. James Buchanan—maybe. Buchanan was the only president who never married. He was bosom friends with another bachelor, William R. King, who was elected vice president on the Franklin Pierce ticket. There was speculation then, and later, that the two men might be "really close," but no one knows for certain.

13. Thomas Jefferson. John Walker challenged Jefferson to a duel, but Jefferson managed to cool his temper.

14. Andrew Jackson—maybe. We know that as overseer of the annual Christmas ball in Salisbury, North Carolina, Jackson impishly invited two prostitutes, who actually did show up.

15. George Washington, who probably got no further than intense flirting.

16. Dwight Eisenhower. Supposedly General George Marshall threatened to make Ike's life miserable if he went through with the scheme. The Eisenhowers deny that Ike ever even contemplated a divorce.

17. James Madison. He was already 31 when he began to pursue her, but she broke off their engagement.

18. Warren Harding. She proved to be quite troublesome, not only for threatening to expose the affair but her outspoken German sympathies during World War I.

19. Lyndon Johnson.

20. Ronald Reagan. They planned to marry but she met someone else, leaving Reagan crushed. Miss Cleaver's name was Margaret, by the way.

21. Gerald Ford. The two planned to marry but she was firm about remaining in New York, while Ford wanted to return to Michigan.

22. Jimmy Carter.

23. James Buchanan, who was engaged to Anne Coleman, daughter of a

very wealthy man. She died suddenly, some said of suicide, and her father would not even let Buchanan attend her funeral. Buchanan's executors destroyed all the papers related to the affair.

24. John F. Kennedy.
25. Donald Trump's mistress (then wife) Marla Maples.

Joining the Club

Most successful politicians are *joiners*. Long before "networking" entered our vocabulary, people running for office understood the importance of belonging to groups—the more the better. Maybe it's because they know Americans like groupy people. Then there's also that basic human need: to meet in groups and enjoy other people's company. As you read the questions below, observe that our presidents' associations have ranged from the sublime to the ridiculous.

1. What booze-loving president joined (but didn't stick with) the Sons of Temperance? (Hint: Civil War)

2. Who, in the 1940s, joined Yale's exclusive Skull and Bones Club?

3. Who joined the Masons in 1752?

4. What unsuccessful president helped found UNICEF and served as honorary chairman of the Boys Clubs of America?

5. What organization uses as its motto a Jefferson quote, "Eternal vigilance is the price of liberty"?

6. What fraternity of Revolutionary War officers made Washington its national president?

7. What Ohio man, a compulsive joiner, belonged to the Masons and also to the Concatenated Order of the Hoo Hoo?

8. Who was made a Sioux chief in 1927?

9. What future president, as a Boys Nation delegate, met John F. Kennedy in 1963?

10. What was the common bond of the Tippecanoe Club that met with Benjamin Harrison in 1888?

11. "Hickory Clubs" were organized to promote the candidacy of what military hero?

12. What Missouri native belonged to (among others) the Masons, the American Legion, and the VFW?

13. What Union veteran and Ohio congressman was active with his wife in the Washington Literary Society?

14. What snobbish New Yorker belonged to the Century Association, which met to discuss Shakespeare and other authors?

15. What extremely intellectual Massachusetts man belonged to the Crackbrain Club?

Joining the Club (answers)

1. Ulysses S. Grant, who definitely did not stick to his pledge of "no liquor." On more than one occasion he marched at the head of a temperance parade.

2. George H. W. Bush.

3. George Washington.

4. Herbert Hoover.

5. The American Civil Liberties Union.

6. The Society of the Cincinnati.
7. Warren Harding. The Hoo Hoo was an order of lumbermen.
8. Calvin Coolidge, who looked embarrassed and silly when photographed in a war bonnet.
9. Bill Clinton.
10. They were all men who had voted for his grandfather, William Henry Harrison, in 1840.
11. Andrew Jackson, "Old Hickory."
12. Harry Truman.
13. James Garfield, who for a time was president of the society.
14. Chester Arthur.
15. John Quincy Adams.

Hobnobbing with the Famous

Ah, the joy of being famous—and of hobnobbing with the famous. In their official capacity, the presidents have rubbed elbows with singers and movie stars, athletes, authors, and Nobel Prize winners. Some of this was pleasant, but then again, the presidents also had to give face time to foreign visitors, stuffed shirts, and . . . well, it isn't *always* a pleasure to meet famous people, is it?

1. In a famous photo, what sexy Hollywood star is draped on a piano that Harry Truman is playing?

2. What hip-swinging Latino singer performed for the George W. Bush inaugural in 2001?

3. What popular black singing group of the 1970s lost some fans when they appeared at the Nixon White House? (Hint: five)

4. Who met with Adolf Hitler in 1938 and watched him go into an anti-Jewish tirade?

5. What hip talk show host had Bill Clinton playing "Heartbreak Hotel" on his saxophone?

6. What aviator hero was the guest of honor at the Coolidge White House?

7. What Democrat hosted Nobel Prize winners at a lavish White House dinner?

8. What Republican went camping with both Thomas Edison and Henry Ford?

9. What handsome, hirsute actor was a noted Reagan supporter, hugging Nancy Reagan at the Republican convention?

10. Who made a short film of buddy William McKinley, the first time a president was filmed?

11. What gutsy man caused controversy by having black leader Booker T. Washington to dinner at the White House?

12. Who, appropriately, received Harriet Beecher Stowe at the White House?

13. What acclaimed female novelist did Theodore Roosevelt invite to the White House to discuss literature?

14. What Revolutionary War hero, a Frenchman, visited the White House and hugged a cordial president?

15. Who sparked controversy by "renting out" the Lincoln Bedroom to generous Democratic contributors?

16. What Republican, in his "front porch" campaign, hosted such big names as Al Jolson, Lillian Gish, and Ethel Barrymore?

17. The Coolidges stayed at San Simeon, the posh California estate of what newspaper mogul?

18. Who was president when Israel's Golda Meir and France's Georges Pompidou visited?

19. What son of a Republican president brought rock stars like George Harrison to the White House?

20. What beloved American poet read his own "The Gift Outright" at John F. Kennedy's inauguration?

21. What mean, gritty boxing champ met with Lyndon Johnson and declared he was ready to "blow this bum off"?

22. Who became the first president to shake the hand of Fidel Castro?

23. What bookish First Couple played hosts to authors Washington Irving and William Makepeace Thackeray, as well as opera singer Jenny Lind?

24. What former military chieftain was White House host to the king of Hawaii and the emperor of Brazil?

25. What wartime First Lady arranged for silent film stars Mary Pickford and Charlie Chaplin to sell Liberty Bonds in Washington?

26. Whose music-loving wife had such White House guests as Al Jolson and pianist Sergei Rachmaninoff?

27. What Republican of the 1930s had Hollywood movie mogul Louis B. Mayer as a guest?

28. What elderly woman painter did the Trumans entertain at the White House?

29. What couple was criticized for serving hot dogs to King George VI of England?

30. What Russian, invited to the Eisenhower White House, was one of the more controversial visitors in the 1950s?

31. Whose White House was host to such musical bigwigs as diva Maria Callas and cellist Pablo Casals?

32. Who had his campaign biography written by novelist Nathaniel Hawthorne, a college buddy?

33. What great American artist was honored by a one-man show at the Nixon White House?

34. Who came to the Rutherford Hayes White House to demonstrate the newly invented phonograph?

35. Who counted millionaires John Rockefeller and Henry Frick among his golfing buddies?

36. What early president corresponded with Daniel Defoe, author of *Robinson Crusoe*?

37. What noted American poet wrote a poem for the White House wedding of Ulysses S. Grant's daughter?

38. Cowboy actor Tom Mix *and his horse* were the guests of what quiet man?

39. What renowned black jazz singer performed at the Johnson White House and got invited to dance by LBJ?

40. Early in the TV era, who used actor Robert Montgomery to coach him on how to behave in front of a camera?

41. What blonde beauty famously sang "Happy Birthday to You" at a party for John F. Kennedy?

42. Swedish soprano Jenny Lind was brought to Millard Fillmore's White House by what renowned American showman?

43. What world leader was Gerald Ford dancing with when the U.S. Marine Band played "The Lady Is a Tramp"?

44. What bereaved First Lady got a condolence letter from Queen Victoria following an assassination?

45. What sort of musicians was Richard Nixon hobnobbing with in 1974 when he performed "God Bless America" on the piano?

46. Who sparred with boxer John L. Sullivan and went hiking with naturalist John Muir?

47. Who, in his days as a diplomat, became close friends with Czar Alexander of Russia?

48. What pop singer of the 1970s danced the "bump" with Betty Ford?

49. Whose 55th birthday party guests included George Lucas and Al Sharpton?

Hobnobbing with the Famous (answers)

1. Lauren Bacall. Truman, vice president at the time, was entertaining servicemen (who probably had their ears on him and their eyes on Bacall).
2. Ricky Martin.
3. The Fifth Dimension.
4. Herbert Hoover, who finally said, "That's enough. I'm not interested in your views."
5. Arsenio Hall.
6. Charles Lindbergh.
7. John F. Kennedy.
8. Warren Harding.
9. Tom Selleck.
10. Thomas Edison.
11. Theodore Roosevelt.
12. Abraham Lincoln. Stowe was the author of the phenomenally popular anti-slavery novel *Uncle Tom's Cabin.*
13. Edith Wharton, author of *Ethan Frome, The Age of Innocence,* and other novels.
14. The Marquis de Lafayette, who was received in 1825 by John Quincy Adams.
15. Bill Clinton.
16. Warren Harding.
17. William Randolph Hearst.
18. Richard Nixon.
19. Jack Ford, son of Gerald, a rock music fan (obviously).
20. Robert Frost.
21. Sonny Liston. At the time of their brief meeting, Johnson was vice president.
22. Bill Clinton.
23. Millard and Abigail Fillmore.
24. Ulysses S. Grant.

25. Edith, second wife of Woodrow Wilson.

26. Calvin Coolidge's.

27. Herbert Hoover.

28. Grandma Moses.

29. Franklin and Eleanor Roosevelt. For the record, the hot dogs (which the king liked) were served at a picnic, not at a formal state dinner. The king also liked FDR's martinis.

30. Nikita Krushchev.

31. John F. Kennedy's.

32. Franklin Pierce.

33. Andrew Wyeth.

34. Its inventor, Thomas Edison.

35. William Howard Taft.

36. Thomas Jefferson.

37. Walt Whitman.

38. Calvin Coolidge.

39. Sarah Vaughan.

40. Dwight Eisenhower.

41. Marilyn Monroe.

42. P. T. Barnum. Though often thought of as a circus promoter, Barnum occasionally added a "class act" like Lind to his list.

43. Queen Elizabeth II.

44. Mary Lincoln.

45. Country music stars. Nixon performed at the dedication of Nashville's new Grand Ole Opry House in January 1974.

46. Theodore Roosevelt, a man of many interests.

47. John Quincy Adams, the first official U.S. minister (ambassador) to Russia. The childless Alexander sometimes got down on all fours to romp with Adams's son.

48. Tony Orlando.

49. Barack Obama. The party was in August 2016.

✷ 3 ✷

Quote, Unquote

Presidents on Presidents

Presidents can be their own worst critics—and the worst critics of other presidents. On the other hand, sometimes they did come up with an occasional word of praise. . . .

1. Who said of his opponent John F. Kennedy, "He seized on every possible shortcoming and inequity in American life and promised immediate cure-alls"?

2. What Republican was Ronald Reagan speaking of when he said, "Look at his record. He cut the taxes four times"?

3. Which early president said of John Adams, "I never felt a diminution of confidence in his integrity"?

4. What 20th-century president said, "James K. Polk, a great president—said what he intended to do and did it"?

5. Who said of Jefferson, "He lives and will live in the memory and gratitude of the wise and good"?

6. Who said of Franklin Pierce, "Our candidate, throughout his life, has proved himself to be peculiarly unselfish"?

7. What future president observed that Ulysses S. Grant, "the honest simple-hearted soldier had not added prestige to the presidential office"?

8. Who said that "Garfield has shown that he is not possessed of the backbone of an angle-worm"?

9. Who said of Benjamin Harrison, "Damn the President! He is a cold-blooded, narrow-minded, prejudiced, obstinate, timid old psalm-singing Indianapolis politician"?

10. Who asked, "What has Grover Cleveland done? Will you tell me?"?

11. Who said of Zachary Taylor, "He was never beaten, and he never retreated"?

12. Which early president said of John Adams, "He and his Federalists wish to sap the Republic by fraud and destroy it by force"?

13. Who said of the assassinated William McKinley, "He has left us a priceless gift in the example of a useful and pure life"?

14. Who said of Warren G. Harding, "He caught the ear of a war-tired world"?

15. Who was Jefferson describing when he said, "Turn his soul wrong side outwards and there is not a speck on it"?

16. Who said of Herbert Hoover, "That man has offered me unsolicited advice for the past six years, all of it bad"?

17. Which future president did George Washington call "the most valuable public character we have abroad"?

18. What president did Lyndon Johnson describe as "the one person I ever knew, anywhere, who was never afraid"?

19. Who said that Dwight Eisenhower was "a far more complex and devious man that most people realized, and in the best sense of those words"?

20. Who described John Quincy Adams as "coarse, dirty and clownish in his address and abstracted in his opinions"?

21. Who stated that Lyndon Johnson was "superficial and opportunistic"?

22. Who said of his mentor Jackson, "I never knew a man more free from conceit"?

23. What Republican described Democrat Woodrow Wilson as "a born crusader"?

24. What early president said of Jackson, "His passions are terrible. . . . He is a dangerous man"?

25. Who said of Theodore Roosevelt, "The eminent fakir can now turn to raising hell, his specialty"?

26. Who described William Henry Harrison as "the greatest beggar and the most troublesome of all the office seekers during my administration"?

27. Who said that Franklin Pierce was "the best-looking President the White House ever had—but as President he ranks with Buchanan and Coolidge"?

28. What president did Theodore Roosevelt say "has no more backbone than a chocolate eclair"?

29. What Democrat described Richard Nixon as "a no-good lying bastard"? (Hint: glasses)

30. What Democrat thanked Gerald Ford "for all he has done to heal our land"?

31. What political enemy's death led John Quincy Adams to describe him as "a hero, a murderer, an adulterer"?

Presidents on Presidents (answers)

1. Richard M. Nixon.
2. Calvin Coolidge.
3. Thomas Jefferson.

4. Harry S. Truman.
5. James Madison.
6. James Buchanan.
7. Woodrow Wilson.
8. Ulysses S. Grant.
9. Theodore Roosevelt.
10. William McKinley.
11. Abraham Lincoln.
12. Thomas Jefferson.
13. Grover Cleveland.
14. Calvin Coolidge, Harding's successor.
15. James Monroe.
16. Calvin Coolidge.
17. John Quincy Adams.
18. Franklin Delano Roosevelt.
19. Richard M. Nixon, his vice president.
20. William Henry Harrison.
21. Dwight Eisenhower.
22. Martin Van Buren.
23. Herbert Hoover.
24. Thomas Jefferson.
25. Warren G. Harding.
26. John Quincy Adams.
27. Harry S. Truman.
28. William McKinley. Later Roosevelt served as McKinley's vice president.
29. Harry S. Truman.
30. Jimmy Carter, Ford's successor.
31. Andrew Jackson.

✷   ✷   ✷

Some Memorable Phrases

American presidents have added more than a few choice phrases to the nation's collective memory. In a few cases (see question 1 below), these were probably phrases the man wishes he'd never uttered.

1. On August 18, 1988, George H. W. Bush said, "Read my lips," followed by what three words?

2. What grinning, spunky president coined the phrase "Speak softly and carry a big stick"?

3. Which Republican president of the 1980s bluntly called the Soviet Union "an evil empire"?

4. What Republican said he was determined "to replace a national frown with a national smile"?

5. What president broke his 1964 campaign promise not to send "American boys to fight Asian wars"?

6. What president claimed to seek "peace with honor" in ending the Vietnam War?

7. What candidate ran in the 1916 presidential race with the slogan "He kept us out of war"?

8. When John F. Kennedy said, "What can you expect from that zoo?" to what was he referring?

9. What tight-lipped president left office in 1929, stating "It's best to get out while they still want you"?

10. On the eve of the Depression, which presidential candidate promised a "chicken in every pot"?

11. What did orphan boy Herbert Hoover describe as "our most valuable natural resource"?

12. What lanky president said, "You can fool all the people part of the time and part of the people all the time, but you cannot fool all the people all the time"?

13. What Republican president announced on taking office in 1974, "Our long national nightmare is over"?

14. Who said, in regard to speechmaking, "Be sincere, be brief, be seated"?

15. What Republican president of the 1970s assured the nation "I am not a crook"?

16. What president wrote the inscription for Sam Houston's gravestone: "The world will take care of Houston's fame"?

17. In 1925 Calvin Coolidge said "The business of America is . . ."—what?

18. Under what frustrated Republican did the word "gridlock" become a fixture in political language?

19. Who was the first president to use the phrase "this nation under God"? (Hint: Civil War)

20. What future president said, during the Revolutionary War, "The united force of Europe will not be able to subdue us"?

21. What president, never liked by liberals, appealed to what he called the "great silent majority of Americans"?

22. Who referred to Islam as "a religion of peace" after a national crisis?

23. What popular president of the 1800s had "Let the people rule" as his slogan?

24. Who was given an unconditional pardon for all crimes "he committed or may have committed" by President Gerald Ford?

25. What early president spoke of "that little spark of celestial fire called Conscience"?

26. Who responded to a Mexican general with the message "Tell him to go to hell"?

27. Who earned himself a nickname during the Civil War when he demanded "no terms except an unconditional and immediate surrender"?

28. What Union veteran defined colonialism as "benevolent assimilation"?

29. What word-happy president lamented politicians' use of "weasel words"?

30. Who drew applause (and hisses) for defining himself as a "compassionate conservative"?

31. What often-used two-word phrase did Warren Harding supposedly coin to refer to the men who started the American republic? (Hint: "F")

Some Memorable Phrases (answers)

1. "No new taxes"—three words he regretted deeply when he lost the 1992 election.

2. Teddy Roosevelt.

3. Ronald Reagan.

4. Gerald Ford.

5. Lyndon Johnson.

6. Richard Nixon.

7. Woodrow Wilson, who, on being re-elected, got the U.S. involved in World War I.

8. Congress.

9. Calvin Coolidge, known as "Silent Cal."

10. Herbert Hoover, who was later to regret that rash promise.

11. Children.

12. Abraham Lincoln. It is probably the best-known presidential quote of all time.

13. Gerald Ford, who proved himself wrong when he issued a pardon to scandal-plagued Richard Nixon.

14. Franklin Roosevelt.

15. Richard Nixon.

16. Andrew Jackson, who had been Houston's military commander.

17. Business.

18. Gerald Ford.

19. Abraham Lincoln. The phrase is in his Gettysburg Address.

20. John Adams.

21. Richard Nixon.

22. George W. Bush, shortly after the attacks on September 11, 2001.

23. Andrew Jackson.

24. Richard Nixon.

25. George Washington.

26. Zachary Taylor, responding to General Santa Ana's demand for surrender.

27. Ulysses S. Grant, who delivered this ultimatum to the Confederates at Fort Donelson in Tennessee. His fans said that "U. S. Grant" stood for "Unconditional Surrender Grant."

28. William McKinley, who happened to be president when the U.S. acquired a *lot* of new territory.

29. Theodore Roosevelt.

30. George W. Bush.

31. Founding Fathers. Harding may not have coined the phrase, but his use of it gave it a wider circulation.

Presidents on the Presidency

For all the effort men put into getting into the White House, you'd think they'd be spouting off about how much they enjoyed their stay there. Not so—most presidents have been happy to *leave* the White House. The comments below are a mix of positive and negative—but definitely weigh in more on the negative side.

1. What general said, "I can command a body of men in a rough way, but I am not fit to be President"?
2. What one-term president admitted that "the presidency is not a bed of roses"?
3. What 20th-century president said the presidency "is preeminently a place of moral leadership"?
4. What military man said, "It was my fortune, or misfortune, to be called to the office of Chief Executive without any previous political training"?
5. Who said to Abraham Lincoln, "My dear sir, if you are as happy on entering the White House as I on leaving, you are a very happy man indeed."
6. What brassy man said that the presidency made "a bully pulpit"?
7. Who said, "I may be President of the United States, but my private life is nobody's damned business"?
8. What portly man said, "I have come to the conclusion that the major part of the President is to increase the gate receipts of expositions and fairs and bring tourists into the town"?
9. Who claimed that "The President is a superior kind of slave, and must content himself with the reflection that the *kind* is superior"?
10. Who told his son, "No man who ever held the office of president would congratulate a friend on obtaining it"?
11. Who said, "My God, this is a hell of a job! I have no trouble with my enemies. But my damn friends, they're the ones that keep me walking the floor at nights"?

12. What unelected president said this: "We elect a man to the presidency, expect him to be honest, to give up a lucrative profession, perhaps, and after we have done with him we let him go into seclusion and perhaps poverty"?

13. Who said he had discovered that "being a President is like riding a tiger. A man has to keep on riding or be swallowed"?

14. Who told listeners that he'd like to "go down in history as the President who made Americans believe in themselves again"?

15. Who said, "To announce that there must be no criticism of the President, or that we are to stand by the President right or wrong, is not only unpatriotic and servile, but is morally treasonable"?

16. What 330-pound president thought so little of his term that he later said, "I don't remember that I ever was president"?

17. Who referred to the White House as "my jail"?

18. Who said—*very* appropriately—"I walk on untrodden ground"?

19. Who said of the White House, "I don't know whether it's the finest public housing in America or the crown jewel of prison life"?

20. What Whig president spoke of his office as "that bed which has afforded me little rest"?

Presidents on the Presidency (answers)

1. Andrew Jackson, who felt himself so unfit that he ran and was elected twice.
2. James K. Polk.
3. Franklin Delano Roosevelt.
4. Ulysses S. Grant.
5. James Buchanan.
6. Theodore Roosevelt.
7. Chester A. Arthur.
8. William Howard Taft.
9. Woodrow Wilson.
10. John Adams, to his newly elected son, John Quincy Adams.
11. Warren G. Harding.
12. Millard Fillmore, who succeeded to the office on the death of Zachary Taylor.
13. Harry S. Truman.
14. Ronald Reagan.
15. Theodore Roosevelt.
16. William Howard Taft.
17. Benjamin Harrison.
18. George Washington, naturally.
19. Bill Clinton.
20. John Tyler.

Those Catty Critics

It's so easy to criticize—particularly when the person you're criticizing can't hunt you down and sue you or beat you to a pulp. The presidents, even the most loved ones, have never lacked for critics. Constant criticism is the flip side of being constantly kowtowed to as "Mr. President."

1. What cowboy comic said of Warren Harding, "I have just read the President's treaty message. I thought it was the best speech Secretary Hughes every wrote"?

2. What consumer advocate said, "Reaganites say that Reagan has lifted our spirits—correct if they mean he led the nation in a drunken world-record spending binge"?

3. Who did columnist Walter Lippman describe as "an indecisive man who lacks that inner conviction and self-confidence which are the mark of the natural leader"?

4. Of whom was Senator Eugene McCarthy speaking when he said, "We've got a wild man in the White House, and we are going to have to treat him as such"?

5. What foreign affairs expert criticized Carter's administration for having "the worst relations with our allies, the worst relations with our adversaries"?

6. Of which president was H. L. Mencken speaking when he said, "If he became convinced tomorrow that coming out for cannibalism would get him the votes he so sorely needs, he would begin fattening a missionary in the White House back yard"?

7. Presidential aide E. M. House said of which president, "He is a timid man frightened into conventionality"?

8. Of whom was Senator Mark Hanna speaking when he said, "Now look! That damned cowboy is President of the United States!"?

9. Who was Robert F. Kennedy speaking of when he said, "He tells so many lies that he convinces himself after a while he's telling the truth"?

10. What Republican candidate said, "I sincerely fear for my country if Jack Kennedy should be elected. The fellow has absolutely no principles"?

11. Columnist Walter Lippman accused which president of having "a vacuum of responsibility and authority"?

12. Who did presidential daughter Alice Roosevelt describe as "not a bad man. He was just a slob"?

13. Who did Senator Timothy Pickering criticize for his "substitution of corruption and baseness for integrity and worth"?

14. What Democrat did journalist Westbrook Pegler say was "afraid to be taken for a valid American"?

15. Of whom did Congressman Joe Cannon say, "He keeps his ear to the ground so close that he gets it full of grasshoppers much of the time"?

16. Which president was the *Chicago Tribune* speaking of in the 1880s when it said, "No president was ever so much given to procrastination as he is"?

17. Republican Senator Robert Taft said of which president, "It defies all common sense to send that roughneck ward politician back to the White House"?

18. Democratic leader Champ Clark said that which president's name deserved to be "linked with Judas Iscariot and Benedict Arnold"?

19. Of which president did Senator Charles Sumner say, "he is an insolent drunken brute, in comparison with which Caligula's horse was respectable"?

20. Of whom did Union general George McClellan say, "The president is nothing more than a well-meaning baboon. He is the original gorilla. What a specimen to be at the head of our affairs now!"?

21. Whom did newspaper publisher Horace Greeley describe as "a good old soul, but don't [sic] know himself from a side of sole leather in the way of statesmanship"?

22. Which president did Whig leader Thurlow Weed describe as a "poor, miserable, despised imbecile, who now goes from the presidential chair scorned of all parties"?

23. Of whom did Congressman Thaddeus Stevens say, "He is dead of lockjaw. Nothing remains but a platform and a bloated mass of political putridity"?

24. To whom did Isaac Milne send a letter saying, "You are perfectly insane and should apply for admission to the lunatic asylum"?

25. Of whom was Benjamin Franklin speaking when he said, "He means well for his country, is always an honest man, often a wise one, but sometimes and in some things absolutely out of his senses"?

26. Of whom did author Ralph Waldo Emerson say, "He could not stand the excitement of seventeen millions of people but died of the Presidency in one month"?

27. Of whom was Mormon leader Brigham Young speaking when he said he "is dead and gone to hell and I am glad of it"?

28. Of whom was Congressman Davy Crockett speaking when he said, "He is laced up in corsets. . . . It would be difficult to say, from his personal appearance, whether he was man or woman"?

29. Which opponent did Henry Clay describe as "ignorant, passionate, hypocritical, corrupt, and easily swayed by the base men who surround him"?

30. Which woman, in a *Newsweek* interview, referred to George W. Bush as the "selected" president?

31. Who did Thomas Paine in an "open letter" accuse of being "treacherous in private friendship . . . and a hypocrite in public life"?

32. Which president did Navy Secretary Gideon Welles refer to as "a political ignoramus"?

33. What wealthy Texan did Texas politician Ann Richards say was "born with a silver foot in his mouth"?

34. What (allegedly) was humorist Dorothy Parker's famous reply when she heard that Calvin Coolidge was dead?

35. What rotund celebrity bashed Obamacare's "clueless planning" and "lousy website"?

36. Who did John F. Kennedy's supporters sometimes refer to as "Uncle Cornpone"?

Those Catty Critics (answers)

1. Will Rogers.
2. Ralph Nader.
3. Richard Nixon.
4. Lyndon Johnson.
5. Henry Kissinger.
6. Franklin D. Roosevelt.
7. Calvin Coolidge.
8. Theodore Roosevelt.
9. Lyndon Johnson.
10. Barry Goldwater.
11. Harry S. Truman.
12. Warren G. Harding.
13. Thomas Jefferson.
14. John F. Kennedy.
15. William McKinley
16. Chester A. Arthur.
17. Harry S. Truman.
18. Grover Cleveland.
19. Andrew Johnson.
20. Abraham Lincoln, McClellan's commander-in-chief.

21. Zachary Taylor, whom Greeley called "Old Zack."
22. John Tyler.
23. James Buchanan.
24. John Quincy Adams.
25. John Adams.
26. William Henry Harrison.
27. Zachary Taylor.
28. Martin Van Buren.
29. Andrew Jackson.
30. Hillary Clinton.
31. George Washington.
32. Ulysses S. Grant.
33. George W. Bush. Even so, in 1994 he defeated Richards in her second run for Texas governor.
34. "How could they tell?"
35. Filmmaker Michael Moore.
36. Lyndon Johnson—JFK's running mate.

Presidents on Themselves

It takes a certain amount of ego to become president, and painfully shy and modest men probably wouldn't want the office at all, would they? So you might think the presidents would have had some grandiose ideas of their own importance, wouldn't you? Some did. But many were surprisingly honest about their shortcomings, either because they know that Americans like modesty and the "Aw, shucks" manner, or because they really were aware of their own failings.

1. What homely president was accused of being two-faced and replied, "If I had two faces, would I be wearing this one"?
2. What chubby man admitted, "There are few people in the world with whom I can converse"?

3. What one-term president predicted (incorrectly) that "history will vindicate my memory"?

4. What quiet man claimed that "Nature intended me for the tranquil pursuits of science, by rendering them my supreme delight"?

5. What military man said, "The truth is, I am more of a farmer than a soldier. I never went into the army without regret and never retired without pleasure"?

6. Who admitted he was "a man of reserved, cold, austere, and forbidding manners"?

7. Who appropriately said, "When I was sixteen, I acted like I was forty, and when I was forty, I acted like I was sixteen"?

8. What bearded Civil War veteran said, "I so much despise a man who blows his own horn that I go to the extreme of not demanding what is justly my due"?

9. What scandal-plagued man once said, "I would have made a good pope"?

10. Who said that "three things can ruin a man—money, power, and women. I never had any money, I never wanted power, and the only woman in my life is up at the house right now"?

11. Who supposedly wrote that limerick that begins, "For beauty I am not a star / There are others more handsome by far"?

12. What 20th-century president described himself as "an idealist without illusions"?

13. Who admitted, in an infamous interview in *Playboy*, that he had "committed adultery in his heart many times"?

14. Who said, "I'm a conservative, but I'm not a nut about it"?

15. What Virginia-born military man laughed at the idea of making a president out of "this clerk and clod-hopper"?

16. What Southerner claimed, with honesty, that as president, he was "the hardest-working man in this country"?

17. What newspaperman claimed that "I am a man of limited talents from a small town"?

18. What man with poor eyesight said of his childhood, "to tell the truth, I was kind of a sissy"?

19. What former college professor claimed that he looked like "an apothecary's clerk"?

20. What Republican made the puzzling remark, "I have opinions of my own—strong opinions—but I don't always agree with them"?

21. What one-term president said, "I am not liked as President by the politicians in office, in the press, or in Congress. But I am content to abide the judgment—the sober second thought—of the people"?

22. What pudgy man confided to his diary, "Vanity is my cardinal vice and cardinal folly"?

23. What Ohio lawyer noted happily that "I always had my plate right side up when offices were falling"?

24. What early president, after acquiring a huge tract of land, admitted he "stretched the Constitution till it cracked"?

25. Who, in one of the most ironic statements ever, pledged that "under no circumstances will I consent to serve a second term"?

26. What honest man, with a scandal-ridden administration, told Congress, "Mistakes have been made"?

27. What lawyer wrote, regarding his possible marriage, "I can never be satisfied with anyone who would be blockhead enough to have me"?

28. What man, with several daughters and no sons, said, "I am submerged in petticoats"?

29. What hulking man said, "Any party which would nominate me would make a great mistake"?

30. Who said, "The American public wants a solemn ass as president, and I think I'll go along with them"?

31. What wealthy man joked, "It's hard nowadays for a man with five children and eleven servants to make a living"?

Presidents on Themselves (answers)

1. Abraham Lincoln.
2. John Adams.
3. James Buchanan. He was wrong, for he is still regarded as one of the most unsuccessful presidents.
4. Thomas Jefferson.
5. Ulysses S. Grant
6. John Quincy Adams.
7. Bill Clinton.
8. James A. Garfield.
9. Richard Nixon.
10. Harry S. Truman
11. Woodrow Wilson. The poem goes on, "But my face I don't mind it / For I am behind it, / It's the people in front that I jar." Wilson was in fact a rather handsome man.
12. John F. Kennedy.
13. Jimmy Carter.
14. George H. W. Bush.
15. William Henry Harrison.
16. James K. Polk, who sometimes did indeed work 14 hours per day.
17. Warren Harding.

18. Harry S. Truman. Because of wearing glasses from an early age, Truman shied away from rough sports.
19. Woodrow Wilson.
20. George H. W. Bush.
21. Rutherford B. Hayes.
22. John Adams.
23. William Howard Taft, whose shape indicated that he *always* had his plate right side up.
24. Thomas Jefferson, who was proud of the Louisiana Purchase but doubtful whether the Constitution gave the president the power to make such a purchase.
25. William Henry Harrison, who lived a bare month after being inaugurated.
26. Ulysses S. Grant.
27. Abraham Lincoln.
28. Woodrow Wilson.
29. William Howard Taft.
30. Calvin Coolidge.
31. Franklin Roosevelt.

✻　　✻　　✻

What the Foreigners Said

Foreigners, particularly Europeans, like to criticize Americans in general, and our leaders in particular. In recent years, the nation as a whole, along with the president, has been called "the Great Satan" in certain locations. Even so, foreign dignitaries have said both good and bad things about our leaders—just as we here at home do the same.

1. What world leader praised Ronald Reagan "for ending the West's retreat from world responsibility, for restoring the pride and leadership of the United States"?
2. What president was Soviet leader Nikita Khrushchev speaking

of when he said, "One shuddered at the thought of what a great force was in such hands"?

3. What president did the emir of Kuwait praise for his "principled, courageous, and decisive position in the face of the Iraqi aggression"?

4. Of whom was French president Georges Clemenceau speaking when he said, "He thinks he is another Jesus Christ come upon the earth to reform men"?

5. Who was novelist Charles Dickens speaking of when he wrote, "His manner was remarkably unaffected. I thought that in his whole carriage he became his station well"?

6. When Fidel Castro of Cuba asked, "How can you take this man seriously?" of what man was he speaking?

7. Who was described by British diplomat Augustus Foster as one who "was allowed on all sides to be a gentleman in his manners as well as a man of public virtue"?

8. Of whom did the Marquis de Lafayette say, "No better minister could be sent to France. He is everything that is good, upright, enlightened, and clever"?

9. What English statesman said that meeting Franklin Roosevelt was like opening one's first bottle of champagne?

10. What president, with his cabinet, did British ambassador Lord Bryce refer to as "the Best and the Brightest"?

11. What man did King William IV of England refer to as "the greatest man who ever lived"?

12. Which Latin American leader, in addressing the United Nations, referred to George W. Bush as "the devil"?

13. What foreign ruler, hearing that George Washington would retire as a farmer after leading the American Revolution, said, "If he does that, he will be the greatest man in the world"?

14. Who was Pope John Paul II speaking of when he said, "I was speaking and he was looking at one of the walls, admiring the frescoes and paintings—he was not listening to me"?

What the Foreigners Said (answers)

1. Margaret Thatcher, British prime minister.
2. Dwight Eisenhower.
3. George H. W. Bush.
4. Woodrow Wilson.
5. John Tyler.
6. Ronald Reagan.
7. James Madison.
8. Thomas Jefferson.
9. Winston Churchill.
10. Theodore Roosevelt.
11. George Washington.
12. Hugo Chavez of Venezuela.
13. George III of England, the king against whom Washington and the other colonists rebelled.
14. Bill Clinton. Meeting with several world leaders, the pope said of the meeting, "The only leader I did not manage to have a proper conversation with was Clinton."

Praising the Presidents, Sometimes Sincerely

Good things are always said at a president's funeral—and that includes some of the comments below. But some of the praise here was said *pre-mortem*. One of the perks of being the top elected official is that someone, somewhere, is always willing to tell you you're a great man.

1. What leader said, "Next to the destruction of the Confederacy, the death of Abraham Lincoln was the darkest day the South has ever known"?

2. Of whom did Mayor Andrew Young of Atlanta say, "If there's one thing could count on ____ for, it's decency and fairness"?

3. Who was described by "Light-Horse Harry" Lee as "first in war, first in peace, first in the hearts of his countrymen"?

4. Which Democratic presidential candidate praised Harry S. Truman for his "candor, honesty, frankness, and principle"?

5. Who was vice president John C. Calhoun speaking of when he said, "Though not brilliant, few men were his equals in wisdom, firmness, and devotion to the country"?

6. Jeane Kirkpatrick, U.S. ambassador to the UN, said that which president brought to the office "confidence in the American experience"?

7. Whom did Senator Ted Kennedy say deserved "a place in the history of civil rights alongside Abraham Lincoln"?

8. Whom did Democratic candidate Alfred E. Smith say belonged to "the class of presidents who were distinguished for character more than for heroic achievement"?

9. To whom did Mark Twain say, "Your patriotic virtues have won for you the homage of half the nation and the enmity of the other half. This places your character upon a summit as high as Washington's"?

10. Who did Chief Justice Earl Warren say was "a fighter for justice, an apostle of peace"?

11. Around which man's memory did Congressman George W. Campbell say "the sons of freedom will rejoice to rally"?

12. Whom did Supreme Court Justice William O. Douglas praise for "his smile and simple frontier approach to complex problems" which "made him as American as apple pie"?

13. Which man did journalist William Allen White describe this way: "I had never known such a man as he, and never shall again. He overcame me"?

14. Which man was Secretary of State John Hay speaking of when he said, "In dealing with foreign power, he will take rank with the greatest of our diplomatists"?

15. Who did poet James Whitcomb Riley praise in these words: "A fearless man inwardly commands respect, and above everything else, _____ was fearless and just"?

16. Who praised Andrew Johnson for being "indifferent to money and careless of praise or censure"?

17. Who did Senator Stephen Douglas describe as "the strong man of his party—full of wit, facts, dates—and the best stump speaker"?

18. Who did novelist Nathaniel Hawthorne say "has in him many of the chief elements of a great ruler"?

19. Who said of Grant, "I have carefully searched the military records of both ancient and modern history, and have never found Grant's superior as a general"?

20. Who did Attorney General John J. Crittenden say he had never heard "utter a foolish or unmeaning word"?

21. Who was described by Confederate general Henry Wise as an "honest, affectionate, benevolent, loving man, who had fought the battles of his life bravely and truly"?

22. Who was Senator Thomas Hart Benton speaking of when he said, "No man could have been more devoted to the Union, or more opposed to slavery agitation"?

23. Which man did author Washington Irving describe as "one of the gentlest and most amiable men I have ever met"?

24. Which man was the *New York Sun* praising in 1849 when it said, "No man and no administration was ever more assailed, and none ever achieved more"?

25. Who did Vice President Aaron Burr praise as "a man of intelligence, and one of those prompt, frank, ardent souls whom I love to meet"?

26. Which man did the World Antislavery Convention of 1843 praise for "the moral heroism" in the anti-slavery cause?

27. Which president did *Collier's Weekly* say had his "distinguished career of public service forgotten in a storm of insult and criticism"?

28. Who was Daniel Webster speaking of when he said, "He has as much to do as any man in framing the Constitution, and as much to do as any man in administering it"?

29. Who did Attorney General Harry Daugherty describe as "a modern Abraham Lincoln, whose name and fame will grow with time"?

30. To whom did Benjamin Rush say, "You stand nearly alone in the history of our public men in never having your integrity called in question or even suspected"?

31. Whom did Governor Nelson Rockefeller describe as "this man of action, this man of accomplishment, this man of courage"?

32. What noted English author spoke of Andrew Johnson as having "one of the most remarkable faces I have ever seen"?

33. Of whom did journalist Mark Sullivan say, "In all three hundred thirty pounds of him, not a pound nor an ounce nor a gram was deceit"?

34. What Oscar-winning actor said, "I'm voting for Barack Obama, 2016. Yes, I am. Four more years"?

Praising the Presidents, Sometimes Sincerely (answers)

1. Confederate president Jefferson Davis.
2. George H. W. Bush.
3. George Washington.
4. Hubert Humphrey.
5. James Monroe.
6. Ronald Reagan.
7. Lyndon Johnson.
8. Calvin Coolidge.
9. Grover Cleveland.
10. John F. Kennedy.
11. Thomas Jefferson.
12. Dwight Eisenhower.
13. Theodore Roosevelt.
14. His boss, William McKinley.
15. His fellow Hoosier, Benjamin Harrison.
16. Jefferson Davis, Confederate president.
17. Abraham Lincoln.
18. His friend Franklin Pierce. The party hired Hawthorne to write Pierce's official campaign biography.

19. Robert E. Lee, who did not live to see that Grant was a better general than a president.

20. Millard Fillmore, his boss.

21. John Tyler, who died after being elected to the Confederate Congress.

22. Zachary Taylor.

23. Martin Van Buren, a fellow New Yorker.

24. James K. Polk.

25. Andrew Jackson.

26. John Quincy Adams.

27. Herbert Hoover, blamed for his handling of the Depression.

28. James Madison.

29. His boss, Warren G. Harding. So far Daugherty's prediction has not come true.

30. John Adams.

31. Richard Nixon.

32. Charles Dickens, who toured the U.S. in 1867-68. Dickens said he was "very much impressed with the President's face and manner."

33. William Howard Taft.

34. Tom Hanks.

Death Sentences: Their Last Words

People's last words fascinate us. They should, particularly in cases where the person appeared to *know* they were saying their last words. See if you can match the president to his dying words.

1. "Thomas Jefferson still survives."

2. "I have a terrific headache." (Hint: handicap)

3. "That is very obvious." (Hint: assassination)

4. "Oh, do not cry. Be good children, and we shall all meet in heaven." (Hint: Tennessee)

5. "I have tried so hard to do right." (Hint: big man)

6. "Please put out the light." (Hint: hunter)
7. "That's good. Go on. Read some more." (Hint: poker)
8. "I am just going. Have me decently buried and do not let my body be put into a vault in less than two days after I am dead? Do you understand me? 'Tis well."
9. "Swaim, can't you stop this? Oh, Swaim?" (Hint: assassinated)
10. "Water." (Hint: Union general)
11. "I want to go. God take me." (Hint: Kansas)
12. "This is the last of earth. I am content."
13. "Is it the Fourth?"
14. "I wish you to understand the true principles of the government. I wish them carried out. I ask nothing more." (Hint: a short term)
15. "I regret nothing, but I am sorry that I am about to leave my friends." (Hint: a general)
16. "Nothing more than a change of *mind,* my dear." (Hint: Virginia)
17. "It is God's way. His will, not ours, be done. Nearer, My God, to thee, nearer to thee." (Hint: assassinated)
18. "I am a broken piece of machinery. When the machinery is broken . . . I am ready." (Hint: professor)
19. "Doctor, I am going. Perhaps it is best."
20. "I know that I am going where Lucy is."
21. "The nourishment is palatable." (Hint: a book-loving New York man)

Death Sentences: Their Last Words (answers)

1. John Adams. As it happened, Jefferson had died hours before, but on the same day, July 4, 1826.
2. Franklin D. Roosevelt.
3. John F. Kennedy. He spoke those words in reply to the wife of John Connally, who had said to him, "You can't say that Dallas doesn't love you."
4. Andrew Jackson.
5. Grover Cleveland.
6. Theodore Roosevelt. He spoke his last words to his valet, then died in his sleep.
7. Warren Harding. His wife had been reading aloud an article about him from the *Saturday Evening Post.*
8. George Washington. His order about waiting two days to bury him stems from the very real fear in those days of being buried alive.
9. James Garfield. David Swaim was his chief of staff. When he pleaded, "Swaim, can't you stop this?" he was referring to the pain he was in.
10. Ulysses S. Grant. Since he died of throat cancer, he could speak little in his last days. Shortly before dying he wrote down these words: "There never was one more willing to go than I am."
11. Dwight Eisenhower.
12. John Quincy Adams, who had a stroke on the House floor and died in the Speaker's chamber. Some witnesses said that his last word was "composed" instead of "content."
13. Thomas Jefferson. He asked the question on July 3, 1826, dying the next day.
14. William Henry Harrison, who died after only a month in office.
15. Zachary Taylor.
16. James Madison. One of his nieces had asked him, "What is the matter, Uncle James?"
17. William McKinley.

18. Woodrow Wilson.
19. John Tyler. After Tyler said, "Doctor, I am going," his doctor had replied, "I hope not, sir."
20. Rutherford Hayes. Lucy was, of course, his late wife.
21. Millard Fillmore, accepting a spoonful of soup.

The Presidential Wit

Wit and folksy humor are something Americans like, and it's hard to imagine us today electing a humorless president. Even in the pre-TV era, Americans liked a "good ole fella" who could make, and take, a joke. Some of their witticisms—sometimes their own, sometimes those of their speechwriters—rank high among "presidential quotables."

1. Who described a radical as "a man with both feet firmly planted—in the air"?
2. What Republican noted that "government always finds a need for whatever money it gets"?
3. What Virginia man said the following: "Popularity may aptly be compared to a coquette—the more you woo her, the more apt is she to elude your embrace"?
4. What former general said that "Fighting battles is like courting girls: those who make the most pretensions and are boldest usually win"?
5. What quiet man noted that "Four-fifths of all our troubles in this life would disappear if we would only sit down and keep still"?
6. Who, having a case of laryngitis, said, "My doctor ordered me to shut up, which will make every American happy"?
7. Who said of a blowhard, "He can compress the most words into the smallest ideas of any man I ever heard"?
8. What Union veteran said that "A pound of pluck is worth a ton of luck"?

9. What dapper man stated that "If it were not for the reporters, I would tell you the truth"?

10. What Democrat defined conservatism as "the policy of' make no change and consult your grandmother when in doubt'"?

11. Who, appropriately, said, "If you don't say anything, you won't be called on to repeat it"?

12. What unpopular Republican said, on the birth of his granddaughter, "Thank God she doesn't have to be confirmed by the Senate"?

13. Who, as a governor of Texas, preached abstinence before marriage but added, "Do as I say and not as I did"?

14. What Texan said, "A town that can't support one lawyer can always support two"?

15. Who noted that "a man who has never gone to school may steal from a freight car, but if he has a university education, he may steal the whole railroad"?

16. Who caused plenty of laughs because he used the word "misunderestimated"?

17. Who, after an assassination attempt, said to his wife, "Honey, I forgot to duck"?

18. What Democrat said, "My choice early in life was either to be a piano player in a whorehouse or a politician, and to tell the truth, there's hardly a difference"?

19. Who threw a huge White House ball just before leaving office and announced, "They cannot say now that I am a president without a party"?

20. What self-taught man stated, "It is a man of small imagination who cannot spell his name more than one way"?

21. What jovial man, inaugurated on a snowy day, noted, "I always said it would be a cold day when I got to be president"?

22. What early president (and vice president) said of the vice presidency, "It will give me philosophical evenings in the winter, and rural days in summer"?

23. What very *un*musical Union veteran claimed, "I know only two tunes—one is 'Yankee Doodle,' and the other isn't"?

24. What academic president said regarding chewing tobacco, "It gives a man time to think between sentences"?

25. When Calvin Coolidge's wife asked him what the minister said about sin in his sermon, what was Coolidge's famous reply?

26. What wealthy Democrat addressed the Daughters of the American Revolution and began by calling them "Fellow immigrants"?

27. What Republican, when asked how he got exercise, replied, "Having my picture taken"?

28. What Democrat, when asked if he played golf, replied that he was "not old enough yet to take up golf"?

29. Who quipped, "I see nothing wrong with giving Robert some legal experience as Attorney General before he goes out to practice law"?

30. What opponent was Lyndon Johnson speaking of when he said, "He wants to repeal the present and veto the future"?

31. Who, when told he was "thin as a shad," replied, "No, even worse—thin as a shadder"?

32. What failed Republican candidate compiled a book titled *Great Presidential Wit*?

The Presidential Wit (answers)

1. Franklin D. Roosevelt.
2. Ronald Reagan.
3. John Tyler.
4. Rutherford Hayes.
5. Calvin Coolidge.
6. Bill Clinton.
7. Abraham Lincoln.
8. James Garfield.
9. Chester Arthur.
10. Woodrow Wilson.
11. The man of few words, Calvin Coolidge.
12. Herbert Hoover.
13. George W. Bush, who had been asked (naturally) if he himself had abstained from sex before he married.
14. Lyndon Johnson.
15. Theodore Roosevelt.
16. George W. Bush.
17. Ronald Reagan, who also said to the doctors attending him, "Please tell me you're all Republicans."
18. Harry Truman.
19. John Tyler, whose party, the Whigs, had largely abandoned him.
20. Andrew Johnson, who was always an indifferent speller.
21. William Howard Taft.
22. Thomas Jefferson.
23. Ulysses S. Grant, who was probably tone-deaf and was not fond of music.
24. Woodrow Wilson.
25. "He was against it."

26. Franklin Roosevelt.

27. Calvin Coolidge.

28. Harry Truman.

29. John F. Kennedy, whose brother Robert served as his Attorney General.

30. Barry Goldwater.

31. Abraham Lincoln.

32. The 1996 Republican candidate, Bob Dole, who, in his post-Washington life, has been a spokesman for both Viagra and Pepsi (hmmm).

Four Quotes on War

1. What Democrat described World War I (wrongly) as "the war to end all wars"?

2. Who, asked how he became a World War II hero, said, "It was involuntary—they sank my boat"?

3. What Virginia gentleman stated that "There is nothing so likely to produce peace as to be well prepared to meet an enemy"?

4. What Civil War veteran observed that "war should never be entered upon until every agency of peace has failed"?

Four Quotes on War (answers)

1. Woodrow Wilson, who obviously did not foresee World War II.
2. John F. Kennedy.
3. George Washington.
4. William McKinley.

Their Occasional Eloquence

Wit is nice, but we still expect the leader of the nation to be, on occasion, eloquent speakers and writers. Some of the most moving phrases in American history came from the presidents—or those in their employment, anyway.

1. Who gave the world such immortal phrases as "life, liberty, and the pursuit of happiness"?
2. What early president warned, "Be courteous to all but intimate with few, and let those few be well tried before you give them your confidence"?
3. Who delivered the brief speech that begins "Four score and seven years ago"?
4. What scholarly man stated that "It is not men that interest or disturb me primarily; it is ideas. Ideas live; men die"?
5. What chubby man said, "Modesty is a virtue that can never thrive in public"?
6. What optimist said, "I believe we can embark on a new age of reform in this country and an era of national renewal"?
7. What Republican claimed that "truth is the glue that holds government together, not only our government but civilization itself"?
8. Who noted that "true Liberalism is found not in striving to spread bureaucracy but in striving to set bounds to it"?
9. What Virginian said, "Surely our government may get on and prosper without the existence of parties"?

10. Who noted that "a brave man is a man who can look the Devil in the face and tell him he is a Devil"?

11. Who told the world that he looked forward to "a world founded upon four essential human freedoms"?

12. What former general warned that "the potential for the disastrous rise of misplaced power exists and will persist"?

13. Who spoke of America as "a thousand points of light in a broad and peaceful sky"?

14. What former general noted that "the great can protect themselves, but the poor and humble require the arm and shield of the law"?

15. What Ohio man said, "Not what a man has, but what he is, settles his class"?

16. Who stated that "a man who has never lost himself in a cause bigger than himself has missed one of life's mountain-top experiences"?

17. What New Yorker observed that "There is a power of public opinion in this country—and I thank God for it"?

18. Who observed that "If the rabble were lopped off at one end and the aristocrat at the other, all would be well with the country"?

19. Who spoke of the quest "not merely for peace in our time, but peace for all time"?

20. Who noted that "the people are the best guardians of their own rights"?

21. Who boasted that "Unlike any other nation, here the people rule, and their will is the supreme law"?

22. What Southern man stated that "We've always had a faith that the days of our children would be better than our own. Our people are losing the faith"?

23. Who observed that "the fundamental trouble with the people of the United States is that they have gotten too far away from Almighty God"?

24. What Republican noted that "the surest way to win the war against poverty is to win the battle against ignorance"?

25. Who, in his last speech before being assassinated, said "Isolation is no longer possible or desirable"?

26. What Virginian claimed the "rebellion to tyrants is obedience to God"?

27. What tiny man wisely observed that "all power in human hands is liable to be abused"?

28. What gutsy character observed that "one man with courage makes a majority"?

29. What small-town laborer claimed that "I desire no better winding sheet than the Stars and Stripes, and no softer pillow than the Constitution"?

30. What one-termer noted that "there is nothing stable but Heaven and the Constitution"?

31. What 20th-century president said, "Let us never negotiate out of fear, but let us never fear to negotiate"?

32. What Tennessee man claimed that "the goal to strive for is a poor government but a rich people"?

33. What military man noted that "There never was a time when some way could not be found to prevent the drawing of the sword"?

34. What very honest man asked, "What is the use of being elected or re-elected, unless you stand for something?"?

35. What Civil War veteran noted that "the manner by which women are treated is a good criterion to judge the true state of society"?

36. What idealistic Democrat believed that "America is the only idealist nation in the world"?

37. What Republican sneered that "almost every Democrat thinks the sovereign remedy for any of our ills is the appropriation of public money"?

38. What honorable (but unsuccessful) president noted that "When there is a lack of honor in government, the morals of the whole people are poisoned"?

39. Who noted that "The ablest man I ever met is the man you think you are"?

40. What ideology did Dwight Eisenhower describe as "global in scope, atheistic in character, ruthless in purpose, and insidious in method"?

41. Who defined tact as "the ability to describe others as they see themselves"?

42. What two-termer said that "America is too great for small dreams"?

43. What Tennessean noted, "I would bring the government back to what it was intended to be—a plain economical government"?

Their Occasional Eloquence (answers)

1. Thomas Jefferson.
2. George Washington.
3. Abraham Lincoln. This is the beginning of his Gettysburg Address.
4. Woodrow Wilson.
5. John Adams.
6. Ronald Reagan.

7. Gerald Ford.
8. Herbert Hoover.
9. James Monroe.
10. James Garfield.
11. Franklin Roosevelt.
12. Dwight Eisenhower.
13. George H. W. Bush.
14. Andrew Jackson.
15. Benjamin Harrison.
16. Richard Nixon.
17. Martin Van Buren.
18. Andrew Johnson.
19. John F. Kennedy.
20. William Henry Harrison.
21. William McKinley.
22. Jimmy Carter.
23. Warren Harding.
24. George H. W. Bush.
25. William McKinley.
26. Thomas Jefferson.
27. James Madison.
28. Andrew Jackson.
29. Andrew Johnson. Appropriately, he was buried with a copy of the Constitution under his head.
30. James Buchanan.
31. John F. Kennedy.
32. Andrew Johnson.
33. Ulysses S. Grant.
34. Grover Cleveland.
35. Benjamin Harrison.

36. Woodrow Wilson.
37. Calvin Coolidge.
38. Herbert Hoover.
39. Franklin Roosevelt.
40. Communism.
41. Abraham Lincoln.
42. Ronald Reagan.
43. James K. Polk.

Inaugural Moments

Beginnings are always interesting, so it's no wonder presidents' inaugural addresses are given a lot of attention . . . even if it turns out the speech was grander than the man himself. Perhaps inaugural addresses might fall into the category of "Good intentions, poor execution" (or "Good talk, bad walk"). On the positive side, many of the presidents (or their writers, anyway) rose to true eloquence in the inaugural speeches.

1. What young president told his fellow Americans, "Ask not what your country can do for you—ask what you can do for your country"?

2. Who, in his first inaugural, spoke of the nation's "arduous struggle for its liberties"?

3. Who promised to try to make government "stand by our side, not ride on our back"?

4. Who (by way of contrast with his predecessor) noted that "a world supergovernment is contrary to everything we cherish"?

5. Who recently began his speech with "This peaceful transfer of authority is rare in history, yet common in our country"?

6. What former general claimed in his inaugural that standing armies are "dangerous to free governments in time of peace"?

7. Who noted that "apprehension seems to exist among the people of the Southern states"?

8. Who spoke of banishing from the land "that religious intolerance under which mankind so long bled and suffered"?

9. What Republican noted that "we cannot learn from one another until we stop shouting at each other"?

10. Who spoke out boldly against "that false philosophy," communism?

11. Which presidents never gave inaugural addresses?

12. Who, in his second inaugural address, criticized the British for helping to arm the Indians?

13. Who observed in his inaugural that "the country having just emerged from a great rebellion"?

14. What former general spoke of the "false and wicked bargain of trading honor for security"?

15. What "good feeling" president praised Americans as "a people so prosperous and happy"?

16. What Northerner claimed in his inaugural that he would support slavery by resisting "the slightest interference with it in the States where it exists"?

17. What great (and egotistical) man informed Americans that "we have become a great nation" among all the other nations?

18. What anti-tax, anti-big-government president assured Americans that "this country believes in prosperity"?

19. Who noted in his first inaugural that "our greatest primary task is to put people to work"?

20. Who, in a long, *long* inaugural, praised the press for protecting freedom of the press and religion?

21. Who placed a *lot* of emphasis in his inaugural on "the Republic of Texas"?

22. What reform-minded Democrat noted that "every citizen owes to the country a vigilant watch and close scrutiny of its public servants"?

23. What New Englander spoke optimistically that, concerning slavery, "I fervently hope that the question is at rest"?

24. What Union veteran soothingly assured Southerners "that it is my earnest desire to regard and promote their truest interest"?

25. Who, in his inaugural, lamented that "geographical parties" had arisen because of the troublesome issue of slavery?

26. Who, in wartime, noted that the recent "tragic events" on the world stage "have made us citizens of the world"?

27. Whose second inaugural contains the famous words "with malice toward none, with charity for all"?

28. Whose inaugural spoke of the "elevation of the negro race from slavery to the full rights of citizenship"?

29. What pudgy man pooh-poohed "ornament and decoration, robes and diamonds" in his one inaugural speech?

30. What president claimed in his inaugural that "the day of the dictator is over"?

31. Who was the only president to speak of "traffic in illegal liquor"?

32. What Democrat spoke of America as "the uncrossed desert and the unclimbed ridge"?

33. What Southerner told Americans that "your strength can compensate for my weakness"?

34. What Republican, at his second inaugural, announced that the U.S. flag was now flying over Cuba, Puerto Rico, and the Philippines?

35. Who encouraged Americans to be "citizens, not spectators" and "citizens, not subjects"?

Inaugural Moments (answers)

1. John F. Kennedy.
2. George Washington. He was speaking, of course, of the American Revolution.
3. Ronald Reagan.
4. Warren Harding, who had no sympathy with Woodrow Wilson and the League of Nations.
5. George W. Bush.
6. Andrew Jackson.
7. Abraham Lincoln. Since the Southern states were already seceding because of his election, he was understating the case.
8. Thomas Jefferson.
9. Richard Nixon.
10. Harry Truman.
11. Those poor vice presidents who became president when the president died in office, but were never elected themselves afterward—namely, John Tyler, Millard Fillmore, Andrew Johnson, Chester Arthur, and Gerald Ford.
12. James Madison. He was speaking of the British in the War of 1812.
13. Ulysses S. Grant.
14. Dwight Eisenhower.
15. James Monroe, whose two terms have often been called the "Era of Good Feelings."
16. Martin Van Buren.
17. Theodore Roosevelt.
18. Calvin Coolidge.
19. Franklin Roosevelt.
20. William Henry Harrison, who, after the longest inaugural address ever, served the shortest presidential term ever.
21. James K. Polk. This was appropriate, since getting Texas into the Union was the key goal of his presidency.

22. Grover Cleveland.
23. Franklin Pierce, in 1853. As history proved, his hopes were dashed.
24. Rutherford Hayes.
25. James Buchanan.
26. Woodrow Wilson.
27. Abraham Lincoln.
28. James Garfield.
29. John Adams. Considering that Adams was rather fond of pomp and ceremony, his speech was rather ironic.
30. George H. W. Bush, who was slightly wrong.
31. Herbert Hoover. Prohibition was repealed under Hoover's successor, FDR.
32. Lyndon Johnson.
33. Jimmy Carter.
34. William McKinley, who was pleased that the Spanish-American War was both short and successful.
35. George W. Bush.

✯ ✯ ✯

Some Memorable Phrases (Part 2)

1. What was the name of the Nashville hotel where Theodore Roosevelt proclaimed the coffee "good to the last drop"?
2. What large item was Ronald Reagan speaking of when he said, "We built it, we paid for it, it's ours, and we're going to keep it"?
3. Who, speaking of people who blamed him for the Depression, said, "I outlived the bastards"?
4. What grinning presidential candidate of the 1970s claimed, "I will never lie to you"?
5. Who pledged himself to "a new deal for the American people"?

6. "The buck stops here" was the motto on which Democrat's desk?

7. What was Dwight Eisenhower speaking of when he said, "This titanic force must be reduced to the fruitful service of mankind"?

8. What early vice president called the office "the most insignificant office that ever the invention of man contrived"?

9. What city did John F. Kennedy describe as having "Southern efficiency and Northern charm"?

10. What Democrat said, "I never trust a man unless I've got his pecker in my pocket"?

11. According to Woodrow Wilson, what war was fought "to make the world safe for democracy"?

12. Who made the phrase "You're fired" part of the TV landscape?

13. Who said that inflation was "public enemy number one" and encouraged people to "Whip Inflation Now"?

14. What Democrat told reporters "Pray for me, boys" when he became president in 1945?

15. Who coined "United Nations"?

16. Who told Mikhail Gorbachev to "tear down this wall"?

17. What four-word phrase did George Washington add to the presidential oath of office?

18. What former military man warned of the dangers of the "military-industrial" complex?

19. Who is sometimes criticized today because he spoke of his affection for his "little brown brothers," the Filipinos?

20. Who supposedly coined the term "muckraker" to refer to investigative reporters?

21. What administrator created the now commonly used word "administrator"?

22. What beloved Democrat supposedly coined this phrase: "When you get to the end of your rope, tie a knot and hang on"?

23. What brassy, outspoken man claimed he was "embarrass-proof"?
24. Who uttered the "Duh!" statement, "When a great many people are unable to find work, unemployment results"?
25. Who supposedly coined "lunatic fringe"?
26. Who criticized small-town Americans for clinging to "guns or religion"?

Some Memorable Phrases (Part 2) (answers)

1. Maxwell House, what else?
2. The Panama Canal.
3. Herbert Hoover.
4. Jimmy Carter.
5. Franklin Roosevelt.
6. Harry S. Truman's.
7. The atomic bomb.
8. John Adams, who was George Washington's vice president and, afterwards, president himself.
9. Washington, of course.
10. Lyndon Johnson, who also said, "If you've got 'em by the balls, their heart and mind will follow."
11. World War I. Wilson had actually borrowed the phrase from author H. G. Wells.
12. Donald Trump, as star of *The Apprentice.*
13. Gerald Ford. "Whip Inflation Now" led to the "WIN" buttons.

14. Harry Truman.
15. Franklin Roosevelt.
16. Ronald Reagan, referring to the Berlin Wall. Reagan got his wish.
17. "So help me God."
18. Dwight Eisenhower.
19. William Howard Taft, who loved his job as governor of the Philippines. Today, many people see "little brown brothers" as condescending.
20. Theodore Roosevelt, supposedly.
21. Herbert Hoover. In his pre-presidential days, Hoover had the federal post of U.S. Food Administrator—Hoover himself recommending the use of the hitherto unused word "administrator." Prior to this, heads of commissions and agencies were generally referred to as "chairmen," not "administrators."
22. Franklin Roosevelt.
23. Harry Truman.
24. Calvin Coolidge.
25. Theodore Roosevelt. If he did not invent the phrase, he did give it wide circulation.
26. Barack Obama, on the campaign trail in 2008. This remark was often referred to as his "guns and God" gaffe.

✳   ✳   ✳

Presidents on Presidents (Part 2)

1. Who accused Jimmy Carter of cooking up "a new and altogether indigestible economic stew"?

2. Who described Gerald Ford as "a nice fellow, but he spent too much time playing football without a helmet"?

3. Who was Jimmy Carter speaking of when he said, "In two hundred years of history, he's the most dishonest President we've ever had"?

4. Who said about Eisenhower, "Ike didn't know anything, and all the time he was in office he didn't learn a thing"?

5. Who said of future president Hoover, "He certainly is a wonder, and I wish we could make him President of the United States. There could not be a better one"?

6. What president was Woodrow Wilson speaking of when he said, "He would rather see a good cause fail than succeed if he were not the head of it"?

7. Who did William Howard Taft describe as "very self-contained, very simple, very direct and very shrewd in his observations"?

8. Who said of Woodrow Wilson, "He is a silly doctrinaire at times and an utterly selfish and cold-blooded politician always"?

9. Whom did Abraham Lincoln describe as "a bewildered, confounded, and miserably perplexed man"?

10. Whom did John Quincy Adams describe as "a barbarian who could not write a sentence of grammar and hardly could spell his own name"?

11. Who, criticizing George W. Bush's foreign policy, said, "This administration has been the worst in history"?

12. Who said of Andrew Johnson, "No man has a right to judge Johnson in any respect who has not suffered as much and done as much as he for the nation's sake"?

13. Who did James Madison say would "live in the memory and gratitude of the wise and good, as a luminary of science, as a votary of liberty, as a model of patriotism"?

14. Whom did Warren Harding refer to as "the little fellow"?

15. Who was Thomas Jefferson speaking of when he said "He is distrustful, obstinate, excessively vain, and takes no counsel from anyone"?

16. What snobbish man wrote in his diary that "Tyler is a political sectarian of the slave-driving, Virginian, Jeffersonian school"?

17. Who wrote of his political opponent William Henry Harrison, "He is as tickled with the presidency as a young man with a new bonnet"?

18. What prudish man described Chester Arthur's White House as "liquor, snobbery, and worse"?

19. What Southern-born president claimed that Grant "combined great gifts with great mediocrity"?

20. What Democrat said of Dwight Eisenhower, "he is just a coward; he hasn't got any backbone at all"?

21. Who was Gerald Ford speaking of when he said "he wants to speak loudly and carry a fly swatter"?

22. To what future president did Andrew Jackson say, "Stop this philandering! You must settle down as a sober married man"?

23. What cabinet member (and future prez) did Warren Harding refer to as "the smartest geek I know"?

24. Who was described by Andrew Johnson as "mendacious, cunning, and treacherous"?

25. What academic spoke of Theodore Roosevelt as "the most dangerous man of the age"?

26. Who referred to his political protégé William Howard Taft as a "fathead"?

27. What Tennessean recalled that some of John Quincy Adams's House speeches were "as fierce as ten Furies"?

28. What Republican said of his successor, "He is the ideal candidate because he is the ideal self-made man"? (Hint: both Union veterans)

29. What Democrat said of the assassinated William McKinley, "All our people loved their dead president"?

30. Whom was Gerald Ford referring to, regarding a potential running mate, when he said, "Absolutely not, I don't want anything to do with that son-of-a-bitch"?

31. What former Coolidge cabinet member wrote that any summation of Coolidge's services to the country must observe "that America is a better place for his having lived in it"?

32. Who, at Harry Truman's funeral, said, "A twentieth-century giant is gone"? (Hint: Texas)

Presidents on Presidents (Part 2) (answers)

1. Ronald Reagan.
2. Lyndon Johnson.
3. Richard Nixon.
4. Harry S. Truman.
5. Franklin D. Roosevelt, who in 1932 defeated Hoover.
6. Herbert Hoover.
7. Calvin Coolidge.
8. Theodore Roosevelt.
9. James K. Polk, who was president when Lincoln served in Congress.
10. Andrew Jackson. This was said before Johnson became president, of course.
11. Jimmy Carter.
12. Abraham Lincoln.
13. Thomas Jefferson.
14. His vice president, Calvin Coolidge.
15. John Adams.
16. John Quincy Adams.
17. Martin Van Buren, whom Harrison defeated.
18. Rutherford Hayes, whose wife Lucy had made the White House an alcohol-free zone.
19. Woodrow Wilson.
20. His predecessor, Harry S. Truman.
21. Jimmy Carter. But the guy with the fly swatter beat Ford in the 1976 election.
22. James K. Polk, who was "Young Hickory" following Jackson as "Old Hickory." Polk took Jackson's advice and married Sarah Childress.
23. His Secretary of Commerce, Herbert Hoover.
24. Ulysses S. Grant. Grant and Johnson definitely did *not* like each other.
25. Woodrow Wilson, who (one suspects) was a bit envious of the vigorous Roosevelt.

26. Theodore Roosevelt. This was *after* he had grown disillusioned with Taft. (Come to think of it, the portly Taft was *literally* a fathead.)
27. Andrew Johnson. Adams's long House career was *after* his presidency.
28. Rutherford Hayes said this of James Garfield.
29. Grover Cleveland.
30. Ronald Reagan.
31. Coolidge's Secretary of State Herbert Hoover.
32. Lyndon Johnson.

✻ ✻ ✻

Presidents on the Presidency (Part 2)

1. What Tennessean stated that "I cannot, whilst president, descend to enter into a newspaper controversy"?

2. What one-termer, a Union vet, noted that "nobody ever left the presidency with less regret, less disappointment, fewer heartburnings"?

3. What man, later assassinated, lamented, "My God! What is there in this place that a man should ever want to get into it?"?

4. What company-loving man said of White House life, "No one ever drops in for the evening"?

5. What modest, quiet man observed that "It is a great advantage to a president for him to know that he is not a great man"?

6. What tough-talking Democrat said "Why in hell does anyone want to be a head of state? Damned if I know"?

7. What cocky young man said, "Sure it's a big job, but I don't know anyone who can do it better than I can"?

8. What blunt speaker from Texas said the presidency was "like being a jackass in a hailstorm"?

9. What New Englander made this White House wish: "May none but honest and wise men ever rule under this roof"?

10. Who said that "the President differs from other men in that he has a more extensive wardrobe"?

11. What nap-loving Republican said of his office, "You go to bed at night knowing that there are things you are not aware of"?

12. What early vice president (and two-term president) said, "The second office of the government is honorable and easy, the first is but a splendid misery"?

13. What frontiersman referred to his presidency as "a situation of dignified slavery"?

14. What brassy New Yorker said this about the White House: "You don't live there. You are only Exhibit A to the country"?

15. What two-term Democrat said, "If you think too much about being re-elected, it is very difficult to be worth re-electing"?

16. What Democrat, when asked why he wanted to be re-elected, glanced around the White House and said, "Where would I ever find another house like this?"?

17. What unsuccessful Republican president said, "This is not a showman's job—you can't make a Teddy Roosevelt out of me"?

Presidents on the Presidency (Part 2) (answers)

1. James K. Polk.
2. Rutherford Hayes.
3. James Garfield.
4. William Howard Taft.
5. Calvin Coolidge.
6. Harry S. Truman.
7. John F. Kennedy.
8. Lyndon Johnson. The quote in full is: "Being president is like being a jackass in a hailstorm. There's nothing to do but stand there and take it."
9. John Adams. (Whether his wish was fulfilled is open to debate.)
10. Herbert Hoover, who, for a Quaker boy, liked to dress well.
11. Ronald Reagan.
12. Thomas Jefferson.
13. Andrew Jackson.
14. Theodore Roosevelt.
15. Woodrow Wilson.
16. Harry Truman.
17. Herbert Hoover.

CHAPTER

✯ 4 ✯

Family Ties

Even Presidents Had Parents

1. What Republican's father was a Wall Street financier and a senator from Connecticut?
2. Whose Missouri-born (and pro-Confederate) mother refused to sleep in the Lincoln bedroom at the White House?
3. What Southerner's mother was known as "Miz Lillian"?
4. How many presidents were posthumous sons (that is, born after the deaths of their fathers)?
5. Whose father, known as "Gus," fathered a president by his second wife, Mary Ball?
6. What Ohio man detested his stepfather, who had divorced his mother in 1848? (Hint: assassination)
7. What wealthy Democrat was an only child?
8. Whose father, named Peter, made a definitive map of the colony of Virginia in 1751?
9. Whose father was an Iowa blacksmith? (Hint: Quaker)
10. Whose wealthy mother had returned from playing golf when she learned of his assassination?
11. Whose devout mother hoped he would be a Quaker missionary?
12. Whose father was an Irish-born Baptist preacher in Vermont and New York?

13. Whose father was a farmer and member of the Texas House of Representatives?

14. What New England president inherited his depression and alcoholism from his mother?

15. What tall president wrote that "all I am or hope to be I owe to my sainted mother"?

16. What hot-tempered frontier president was an orphan at age fourteen?

17. Who had a wealthy New Yorker father and a Georgia plantation belle mother?

18. What tip-lipped president carried a picture of his beloved mother Victoria in his watch-case?

19. Whose father was Benjamin Harrison V, "the Signer"?

20. How many presidents were PKs (preacher's kids)?

21. What president and Virginia governor had a father who was Virginia governor from 1809 to 1811?

22. What devout mother was so well-loved that her son raced from Washington to Ohio to be with her when she died?

23. Who admitted he was a "mama's boy," overly fond of his English-born mother? (Hint: glasses)

24. What Tennessee woman was the first presidential mother to outlive her son?

25. What Ohio man declined his share of his father's wealth?

26. What New Yorker was the first president to have his father visit him in the White House?

27. Whose Irish-born father immigrated to Pennsylvania in 1783?

28. Whose pa was a Presbyterian parson in Virginia, New Jersey, and New York?

29. What prairie lawyer did not bother to attend his father's funeral, less than fifty miles away?

30. Whose father was a president's son?

31. What Virginia-born president was son of a Presbyterian pastor and seminary professor?

32. What military man was the son of a pacifist mother who wept when he went off to West Point?

33. Who had the presidential oath of office administered by his own father?

34. Whose widowed mother was a Quaker preacher and women's rights advocate? (Hint: Iowa)

35. Who, after his parents' divorce, had an Indonesian stepfather?

36. Whose mother begged him to retire from public life after disability struck him?

37. What Ohio man's father married three wives, one when he was sixty-eight, another when he was seventy-eight? (Hint: died in office)

38. What wealthy Bostonian was the first presidential father to attend his son's D.C. inauguration?

39. What portly man's father was Grant's Secretary of War and an ambassador to Russia?

40. The woman born Abigail Smith was the wife and mother of which two presidents?

41. Whose father was a California gas station owner?

42. Whose remarkable mother, Nelly Rose Conway, lived to be 98 and to the end could read without glasses? (Hint: Virginia)

43. What Republican could recall meeting his biological father only twice?

44. What New England man described his father, born in 1691, as "the honestest [sic] man I ever knew"?

45. Whose Illinois-born father was a shoe salesman with a sixth-grade education?

46. What presidential mom, from Kennebunkport, Maine, was an avid tennis and softball player?

47. What supposedly "uptight" president would kiss his father whenever they met?

48. What frontier boy grew up listening to his mother's stories of tyrannical rule in Ireland?

49. Whose widowed mother moved to Boston to be near him in his Harvard days?

50. Whose Scottish-born mother entered the U.S. on her 18th birthday?

51. Of which two famous Pilgrims were John Adams and John Quincy Adams descendants? (Hint: a Longfellow poem)

Even Presidents Had Parents (answers)

1. George H. W. Bush. His father was Prescott Bush.

2. Harry Truman's. His mother, Martha Ellen Truman, had childhood memories of suffering at Yankee hands, so anything connected with Lincoln was unpleasant to her.

3. Jimmy Carter.

4. Andrew Jackson, Rutherford Hayes, and Bill Clinton.

5. George Washington, whose father's full name was Augustine.

6. James A. Garfield.

7. Franklin Roosevelt. Technically, FDR did have a half-brother from his father's first marriage.

8. Thomas Jefferson.

9. Herbert Hoover. His father, Jesse Clark Hoover, died when the boy was six.

10. Rose Kennedy, mother of John.

11. Richard Nixon.

12. Chester A. Arthur.

13. Lyndon Johnson.

14. Franklin Pierce, who had the weaknesses of his mother, Anna Kendrick Pierce.

15. Abraham Lincoln, paying tribute to Nancy Hanks Lincoln.

16. Andrew Jackson.

17. Theodore Roosevelt. His mother, "Mittie," openly supported the Confederate cause during the Civil War.

18. Calvin Coolidge.

19. William Henry Harrison. His father was a signer of the Declaration of Independence.

20. Chester Arthur, Grover Cleveland, and Woodrow Wilson.

21. John Tyler.

22. William McKinley's mother Nancy.

23. Woodrow Wilson.

24. Jane Knox Polk, mother of James K. Polk.

25. Ulysses S. Grant, who was not close to his father, Jesse Root Grant.

26. Millard Fillmore.

27. James Buchanan.

28. Grover Cleveland.

29. Abraham Lincoln, who apparently was not close to his father Thomas.

30. Benjamin Harrison, whose father John Scott Harrison, was son of William Henry Harrison.

31. Woodrow Wilson.

32. Dwight Eisenhower.

33. Calvin Coolidge. His father was both a notary and a justice of the peace.

34. Herbert Hoover.

35. Barack Obama.

36. Franklin Roosevelt.

37. Warren Harding.
38. Joseph P. Kennedy, father of John.
39. William Howard Taft. His father's name was Alphonso.
40. She was the wife of John Adams, mother of John Quincy Adams.
41. Richard Nixon.
42. James Madison.
43. Gerald Ford. His actual father, Leslie King, divorced his mother when the child was three, and saw his son twice after the divorce. Ford was given the name of his adoptive father and did not know he was adopted until he was twelve.
44. John Adams.
45. Ronald Reagan. His father was named Jack.
46. Dorothy Bush, mother of George H. W. Bush.
47. Calvin Coolidge.
48. Andrew Jackson, whose parents both came from northern Ireland.
49. Franklin Roosevelt's.
50. Donald Trump's mother, Mary MacLeod Trump.
51. John Alden and Priscilla Mullins, made famous in Longfellow's poem *The Courtship of Miles Standish.*

✳   ✳   ✳

My Mom and Dad Were . . .

1. Prescott S. _____ and Dorothy Walker
2. Jack _____ and Nelle Wilson
3. Frank Anthony _____ and Hannah Milhous
4. James Earl _____ Sr. and Lillian Gordy
5. Joseph P. _____ and Rose Fitzgerald
6. James _____ and Sara Delano
7. George T. _____ and Phoebe Elizabeth Dickerson
8. Sam Ealy _____ and Rebekah Baines
9. Theodore _____ and Martha Bulloch

10. Abram _____ and Eliza Ballou
11. Andrew _____ and Elizabeth Hutchinson
12. Augustine _____ and Mary Ball
13. Jesse _____ and Hannah Simpson
14. Alphonso _____ and Louisa Torrey
15. John Calvin _____ and Victoria Josephine Moor
16. Thomas _____ and Nancy Hanks
17. John Scott _____ and Elizabeth Irwin
18. Benjamin _____ and Anna Kendrick
19. John _____ and Susanna Boylston
20. John _____ and Mary Armistead
21. Rutherford _____ and Sophia Birchard
22. Joseph Ruggles _____ and Jessie Woodrow
23. John Anderson _____ and Martha Ellen Young
24. William _____ and Nancy Allison
25. William _____ and Malvina Stone
26. Peter _____ and Jane Randolph
27. Abraham _____ and Maria Hoes
28. James _____ and Elizabeth Speer
29. James _____ and Nelly Conway
30. Samuel _____ and Jane Knox
31. Nathaniel _____ and Phoebe Millard
32. Jacob _____ and Polly McDonough
33. Jesse Clark _____ and Huldah Minthorn
34. Spence _____ and Elizabeth Jones
35. Rev. Richard _____ and Ann Neal
36. George H. W. _____ and Barbara Pierce
37. Barack _____ and Ann Dunham
38. David Jacob _____ and Ida Elizabeth Stover
39. John _____ and Abigail Smith

40. Benjamin _____ V and Elizabeth Bassett
41. William Jefferson Blythe III and Virginia Kelley
42. Richard _____ and Sally Dabney Strother
43. Leslie Lynch King and Dorothy Gardner
44. Frederick _____ and Mary Anne MacLeod.

My Mom and Dad Were . . . (answers)

1. George H. W. Bush.
2. Ronald Wilson Reagan.
3. Richard Milhous Nixon.
4. James Earl (Jimmy) Carter, Jr.
5. John Fitzgerald Kennedy.
6. Franklin Roosevelt.
7. Warren Harding.
8. Lyndon Baines Johnson.
9. Theodore Roosevelt.
10. James Garfield.
11. Andrew Jackson.
12. George Washington.
13. Ulysses S. Grant.
14. William Howard Taft.
15. Calvin Coolidge.

16. Abraham Lincoln.
17. Benjamin Harrison.
18. Franklin Pierce.
19. John Adams.
20. John Tyler.
21. Rutherford Hayes.
22. Woodrow Wilson.
23. Harry Truman.
24. William McKinley.
25. Chester Arthur.
26. Thomas Jefferson.
27. Martin Van Buren.
28. James Buchanan.
29. James Madison.
30. James Knox Polk.
31. Millard Fillmore.
32. Andrew Johnson.
33. Herbert Hoover.
34. James Monroe.
35. Grover Cleveland.
36. George W. Bush.
37. Barack Obama.
38. Dwight Eisenhower.
39. John Quincy Adams.
40. William Henry Harrison.
41. Bill Clinton, who took his last name from his adoptive father.
42. Zachary Taylor.
43. Gerald Ford, whose name was that of his adoptive father. His birth name was in fact Leslie Lynch King, Jr.
44. Donald Trump.

Getting Born: Log Cabins, and All That

1. Who was born at his family's estate on the south side of the Potomac?

2. Who, born in Brookline, Massachusetts, was the first president born in the 20th century?

3. Which two Southern states claim to be the birthplace of Andrew Jackson?

4. Whose birth at a New York estate nearly killed him and his mother?

5. What military man, who campaigned as a "log cabin" candidate, was actually born in a Virginia plantation house?

6. How many presidents were born in parsonages?

7. Who was born above a bakery in Tampico, Illinois?

8. Who was born in a log cabin in Raleigh, North Carolina, but is most often associated with Tennessee?

9. Which presidents were actually born in log cabins?

10. What Virginian was born at a plantation called Shadwell?

11. What Republican was a real Yankee Doodle Dandy, born on the 4th of July (in Vermont)?

12. Who was born at a James River plantation called Greenway?

13. What future general was born near the Ohio River at Point Pleasant?

14. Who was born to wealth in a New York brownstone?

15. Who was born in a dirt-floor log cabin in Larue County, Kentucky?

16. What president, the last log-cabin birth, was born in Orange, Ohio?

17. Who was born in the Ohio home of another future president?

18. What military man was born in western Virginia but grew up in Kentucky?

19. Who was born in Staunton, Virginia, and lived in the South during Civil War and Reconstruction?

20. Who was born in California in a house his father had built?

21. Who was born to a Quaker family in a modest home in Iowa?

22. Who was born literally on "the other side of the tracks" in Denison, Texas?

23. Who was born in a Texas farmhouse in a town named for his grandfather?

24. What Pennsylvanian was born in a log cabin in Cove Gap?

25. What was the distinction of Jimmy Carter's birth in Wise Hospital, Plains, Georgia?

26. What New England-born president was, his critics said, actually born in Canada?

27. Who was born in Milton, Massachusetts, grew up in Connecticut, but made his reputation in Texas?

Getting Born: Log Cabins, and All That (answers)

1. George Washington, of course.

2. John F. Kennedy.

3. North and South Carolina. The Waxhaw region where he was born lies astraddle the two states. Jackson himself believed he was born in South Carolina.

4. Franklin Roosevelt. The newborn FDR had to be given mouth-to-mouth resuscitation.

5. William Henry Harrison.

6. Parsonages are ministers' homes. The presidents born in parsonages were Chester Arthur, Grover Cleveland, and Woodrow Wilson.

7. Ronald Reagan.

8. Andrew Johnson.

9. Andrew Jackson, James K. Polk, Millard Fillmore, Franklin Pierce, James Buchanan, Abraham Lincoln, Andrew Johnson, and James Garfield.

10. Thomas Jefferson.

11. Calvin Coolidge.

12. John Tyler.

13. Ulysses S. Grant.

14. Theodore Roosevelt.

15. Abraham Lincoln.

16. James Garfield.

17. Benjamin Harrison, born at the home of his grandfather William Henry Harrison.

18. Zachary Taylor.

19. Woodrow Wilson. Both Wilson's parents were staunch supporters of the Confederacy.

20. Richard Nixon.

21. Herbert Hoover.

22. Dwight Eisenhower. The family was in a rented room near the railroad tracks.

23. Lyndon Johnson, born near Johnson City.

24. James Buchanan.

25. The first president born in a hospital.

26. Chester Arthur, born in Vermont. His father had lived awhile in Canada. Arthur's enemies were trying to make the case that he could not serve as president since a president must be native-born.

27. George H. W. Bush.

✳   ✳   ✳

The Birth Order Questions

Why do people ask "What's your sign?" when a much more revealing question is "Where did you fall in your family's birth order?" Some truisms are, well, true—such as, that firstborn sons are usually the more mature and successful, the youngest child is often bratty and immature, an only child is often self-centered, and . . . well, there are always exceptions.

By the way, and for what it's worth: quite a few of the presidents came from *large* families.

1. How many presidents were the oldest sons in their families?
2. Which president was an only child?
3. And which presidents were the youngest children in their families?
4. Which president (who was, ironically, childless) was from a family of ten siblings?

The Birth Order Questions (answers)

1. John Adams, Jefferson, Madison, Monroe, John Quincy Adams, Polk, Fillmore, Buchanan, Lincoln, Grant, Hayes, Theodore Roosevelt, Wilson, Harding, Coolidge, Franklin Roosevelt, Truman, LBJ, Ford, Carter, George W. Bush. In other words, half the men to hold the office were oldest sons. (Can we draw any lessons from this?)

2. Franklin Roosevelt. Technically he wasn't, for he had a much older half

brother (from his father's first marriage), but FDR was definitely *raised* as an only child.

3. William Henry Harrison and James Garfield. Sometimes the baby in the family does rise to high office. Ironically, both these men died soon after becoming president.

4. James K. Polk. This was the largest brood for the raising of a future president. (Note: when counting the presidents' brothers and sisters, the historians have to add "those who survived past infancy." Infant mortality was high in the 1800s.)

Brothers and Sisters

1. What Southerner's younger brother had a beer named for him?

2. What early president from Virginia had his older half-brother Lawrence as a surrogate father?

3. What Democrat's siblings included two senators, an Attorney General, a mentally retarded woman, and the wife of a noted actor?

4. What Southern frontiersman had two Irish-born brothers who died fighting in the American Revolution?

5. What Republican had five brothers, all of whom went by the same nickname?

6. What recent Republican's brothers include three wealthy businessmen?

7. Who had a wayward younger brother named Elliot who was father of a First Lady?

8. What bachelor president had two bachelor brothers?

9. Who had four brothers, one of whom sold hamburgers named for the family? (Hint: California)

10. Who has an older brother named "Moon"? (Hint: California, again)

11. Who had a minister brother who married the sister of songwriter Stephen Foster? (Hint: bachelor)

12. Who has a musician half-brother named Roger?

13. What New Englander claimed he entered politics "because Joe died," referring to his older brother?

14. What Democrat had a brother named Vivian?

15. Who, as governor of a large state, was elected president while his brother was governor of Florida?

16. Who had eight half-siblings?

Brothers and Sisters (answers)

1. Jimmy Carter. Billy will probably be best remembered for Billy Beer.

2. George Washington.

3. John F. Kennedy, who was one of nine children.

4. Andrew Jackson.

5. Dwight Eisenhower, who, like his brothers, got the nickname "Ike."

6. George H. W. Bush.

7. Theodore Roosevelt. Elliot's daughter Eleanor married Franklin Roosevelt.

8. Grover Cleveland. Unlike his two brothers, however, he did not *remain* a bachelor.

9. Richard Nixon. His brother Donald ran a drive-in chain that sold Nixonburgers.

10. Ronald Reagan. His older brother's real first name is Neil.

11. James Buchanan.

12. Bill Clinton.

13. John F. Kennedy, who, as the surviving oldest son, felt pressured by his father to enter politics and eventually become president.

14. Harry Truman.

15. George W. Bush. Brother Jeb was governor of Florida, George of Texas.

16. Barack Obama, whose siblings' history is, to put it mildly, complicated.

Presidential Progeny

Ah, the joys of childrearing . . . well, sometimes. Some presidential kids have made their papas proud, while others have embarrassed the whole nation. What is true of presidential progeny is true of children in general: a mixed bag.

1. Who had a beloved son nicknamed "Tad"?

2. Who holds the record—fourteen—for having the most children? (Hint: Virginia)

3. Which presidents were childless?

4. Who said of his oldest daughter, "I can be president of the United States, or I can control Alice—I cannot possibly do both"?

5. What childless Virginian adopted his wife's two children from her first marriage?

6. Who was not only a president and father of a president, but the ancestor of a noted New England political clan?

7. What frontier president adopted his wife's nephew as his legal son?

8. Who put his two daughters in a Paris convent school while he lived in France?

9. Who had a daughter that married—much against his will— Jefferson Davis?

10. What early president named his first son for Washington?

11. What ex-president simultaneously had two sons serving as state governors?

12. Who was father of the only child born in the White House?

13. Whose daughter was married to Senator Chuck Robb of Virginia?

14. What son of a president brought rock stars like George Harrison to the White House?

15. Who had two daughters by his wife Ida, with both daughters dying as infants?

16. Whose son Robert became "Mr. Republican" in the U.S. Senate?

17. Who was (supposedly) father of Maria Halpin's son Oscar?

18. What president, born in 1790, still has a *grandson* living?

19. Which family has had three generations serving as ambassadors to Great Britain?

20. What president's son joined the Union army just before the Civil War ended?

21. Whose children played host to the children in the first White House Easter egg roll?

22. What singer performed with the Detroit Symphony and made her television debut on the Ed Sullivan show?

23. Who was the only child of a president to die in the White House?

24. For whose child was the "Baby Ruth" candy bar named?

25. Whose son Robert served as his father's secretary while president but embarrassed the family with his drinking?

26. Whose daughter was arrested for protesting outside the South African embassy?

27. What presidential daughter was known in the press as "Washington's other monument"?

28. Whose only child died just a few weeks before the presidential inauguration?

29. Whose beloved son Quentin was shot down by German fighters during World War I?

30. What president's daughter became a devotee of an Indian religion and took an Indian name?

Presidential Progeny (answers)

1. Abraham Lincoln. He called his son Thomas "Tad" because he said he looked like a tadpole.

2. John Tyler, who was married twice. Tyler himself was from a family of eight children.

3. George Washington, James Madison, Andrew Jackson, James K. Polk, James Buchanan, and Warren Harding (although Harding quite possibly fathered at least one illegitimate child).

4. Theodore Roosevelt. Alice was as high-spirited as her father.

5. George Washington. Martha had two children by her first husband. The two were John Parke Custis and Martha Parke Custis.

6. John Adams, father of John Quincy Adams and ancestor of many noted Adamses in American history.

7. Andrew Jackson, who legally adopted his wife Rachel's nephew, one of two twin boys born to her brother. The boy was legally named Andrew Jackson, Jr.

8. Thomas Jefferson, who was ambassador to France for several years.

9. Zachary Taylor. Sarah Knox Taylor, known as "Knoxie," eloped, but died shortly after the wedding. Davis and Taylor later became friends.

10. John Quincy Adams, who named his eldest George Washington Adams.

11. George H. W. Bush, whose son Jeb was governor of Florida while George W. was governor of Texas.

12. Grover Cleveland. His daughter Esther was born there in 1893.

13. Lyndon Johnson, whose daughter Lynda Bird married Robb in 1967.

14. Jack Ford, son of Gerald, a rock music fan (obviously).

15. William McKinley.

16. William Howard Taft. Robert Alphonso Taft was a Senate powerhouse for years and nearly won the 1952 presidential nomination, though was beat out by Eisenhower.

17. Grover Cleveland. He had "kept company" with Miss Halpin in his bachelor days, and in September 1874 she gave birth to son she named Oscar Folsom Cleveland, claiming Grover Cleveland as the father. The mother was a problem drinker, and she spent some time in an asylum. Cleveland supported the boy, who eventually became a doctor.

18. John Tyler. This seems bizarre until we recall that John was still fathering children at the age of 70. The grandson still lives at the family home in Virginia.

19. The Adamses. John Adams, his son John Quincy Adams, and grandson Charles Francis Adams all served in Britain.

20. Abraham Lincoln's. His oldest son Robert was present at the Appomattox surrender.

21. Rutherford Hayes's youngest children, Scott and Fanny.

22. Margaret Truman, only child of Harry S.

23. William "Willie" Lincoln, second son of Abraham. He died in 1862, causing incredible grief to Abraham and especially to Mary.

24. Grover Cleveland. Ruth Cleveland, born in 1891, died at age 12.

25. Andrew Johnson's. Robert died in 1869.

26. Jimmy Carter. His daughter Amy was arrested in 1985.

27. Catty, gossipy Alice Roosevelt Longworth, daughter of Theodore. She died at age 96 and was known as a sharp-witted hostess.

28. Franklin Pierce. The death of his son Bennie was a blow from which his wife Jane never recovered. Bennie was the only fatality in a train accident.

29. Theodore Roosevelt.
30. Woodrow Wilson. His daughter Margaret moved to India and took the name Dishta. Curiously, her earlier career was as a singer.

Who Was My Dad?

Name the president after reading the list of his offspring.

1. Maureen, Michael, Patricia, Ron
2. Chelsea
3. Abigail, Susanna, John Quincy, Charles, Thomas
4. Eliza, Harry, James, Mary, Irvin, Abram, Edward
5. Robin, George, Jeb, Neil, Marvin, Dorothy
6. George, John, Charles, Louisa
7. Patsy, Polly
8. Abraham, Martin, John, Smith
9. Robert, Edward, William, Tad
10. Alice, Kermit, Ethel, Archibald, Quentin, Theodore
11. Doud, John
12. Robert, Helen, Charles
13. Frederick, Ellen, Jesse, Ulysses
14. Mary, Millard
15. Jessie, Eleanor, Margaret
16. John, Franklin, Elliot, James, Anna
17. Ruth, Esther, Marion, Richard, Francis
18. Benjamin, Franklin
19. Mary, Robert, John, Letitia, Elizabeth, Anne, Alice, Tazewell, David, Julia, Lachlan, Lyon, Pearl
20. John, Amy, Chip, Jeffrey
21. John, Calvin
22. Luci, Lynda

23. Knox, Anne, Octavia, Mary, Margaret, Elizabeth, Richard
24. Eliza, Maria
25. Russell, Mary, Elizabeth
26. Jenna, Barbara (twins)
27. Sardis, James, Joseph, George, Fanny, Scott, Manning, Rutherford
28. Lucy, John Scott, Benjamin, Mary, Carter, Anna, James, John Cleves
29. Katherine, Ida
30. Julie, Patricia
31. Martha, Charles, Mary, Robert, Andrew
32. John, Caroline, Patrick
33. Margaret
34. Ivanka, Eric, Tiffany, Barron, Donald
35. Allan, Herbert
36. Steve, Michael, Susan, John
37. Malia, Sasha

Who Was My Dad? (answers)

1. Ronald Reagan.
2. Bill Clinton.

3. John Adams.
4. James Garfield.
5. George H. W. Bush.
6. John Quincy Adams.
7. Thomas Jefferson.
8. Martin Van Buren.
9. Abraham Lincoln.
10. Theodore Roosevelt.
11. Dwight Eisenhower.
12. William Howard Taft.
13. Ulysses S. Grant.
14. Millard Fillmore.
15. Woodrow Wilson.
16. Franklin Roosevelt.
17. Grover Cleveland.
18. Franklin Pierce.
19. John Tyler.
20. Jimmy Carter.
21. Calvin Coolidge.
22. Lyndon Johnson.
23. Zachary Taylor.
24. James Monroe.
25. Benjamin Harrison.
26. George W. Bush.
27. Rutherford Hayes.
28. William Henry Harrison.
29. William McKinley.
30. Richard Nixon.
31. Andrew Johnson.
32. John F. Kennedy.

33. Harry Truman.
34. Donald Trump.
35. Herbert Hoover.
36. Gerald Ford.
37. Barack Obama.

✷　✷　✷

Presidential Progeny (Part 2)

1. What Republican fathered the "love child" Elizabeth Ann Christian?
2. Whose son died from a toe infection while his father faced an election year? (Hint: quiet)
3. What engineer had two sons who both became engineers?
4. What Democrat's son published a 1974 memoir that irked his brothers and sisters?
5. Whose son became a noted Confederate general and historian of the Civil War?
6. What protective father told a music critic he'd like to punch him in the nose and the groin? (Hint: glasses)
7. Whose handsome son died in a plane crash off the Massachusetts coast?
8. Whose daughter-in-law served as White House hostess?
9. What presidential daughter dated the ever-tan actor George Hamilton?
10. Whose daughter married the grandson of Dwight Eisenhower?
11. Whose oldest child Martha served as White House hostess during his term?
12. Which president had a son who was a cast member on *The Young and the Restless*?
13. Who fathered a daughter when he was 64?
14. Who is the father of actress Jane Wyman's daughter?

15. What governor converted to Catholicism under the influence of his Mexican-born wife Columba?

16. How many presidents have fathered sons who were "Juniors"?

17. What Republican claimed that his greatest success in life was that his children "still come home"?

18. Whose household included not only his wife's two children, but two grandchildren as well?

19. What diplomat's daughter attended a posh girls' school with the stepdaughter of Napoleon?

20. What widowed president proposed to Ellen Randolph, the granddaughter of Thomas Jefferson?

21. What Virginia-born man had only two of his ten children live to the age of forty?

22. Who has twin daughters, Jenna and Barbara, named for their grandmothers?

23. What Virginian had so many children that they formed a family orchestra?

24. What Democrat had his campaign plane named for his young daughter?

25. Whose son was at the scene of three presidential assassinations?

Presidential Progeny (Part 2) (answers)

1. Warren Harding, or so we believe. She was the daughter of his affair with young Nan Britton. Harding had child support sent to Nan via Secret Service agents. Supposedly Harding arranged trysts with Nan even at the White House.

2. Calvin Coolidge. His son, Calvin, Jr., injured his toe while playing tennis, and somehow the infection led to his death at age 16. Both parents were devastated.

3. Herbert Hoover.

4. Elliott Roosevelt, son of Franklin. The book was *An Untold Story: The Roosevelts of Hyde Park.*

5. Zachary Taylor, whose son Richard was the last Confederate general to lay down his arms. His memoirs, *Destruction and Reconstruction,* are still widely read.

6. Harry Truman, who reacted to a music critic who said some negative things about the singing of daughter Margaret Truman. Harry fired off his infamous letter to the critic, saying that any good father would do the same.

7. John F. Kennedy. John Jr.'s death was quite a shock to the nation.

8. William Henry Harrison's. Jane Irwin Harrison was the widow of his deceased son, William Jr.

9. Lynda Bird Johnson, daughter of Lyndon.

10. Julie Nixon, daughter of Richard. She married David Eisenhower II in 1968. The marriage is interesting, since her father served as vice president when her husband's grandfather was president.

11. Andrew Johnson. His wife Eliza was an invalid, and Martha did fine as hostess.

12. Gerald Ford, whose son Steven Meigs Ford is an actor.

13. Benjamin Harrison, who at age 62 took his second wife, who was 37.

14. Ronald Reagan, father of Maureen Reagan.

15. Jeb Bush of Florida, son of George H. W. Bush.

16. Eleven—which says something about the male ego. Those eleven:

Van Buren, W. H. Harrison, Tyler, Andrew Johnson, Grant, Arthur, T. Roosevelt, Coolidge, Hoover, FDR, and JFK. The total is twelve if we count Andrew Jackson, Jr., who was an *adopted* son. Jimmy Carter, who is James Earl Carter, Jr., has a son "Chip" who is James Earl Carter III. George H. W. Bush's son George W. Bush is technically not a Jr.

17. George H. W. Bush.

18. George Washington. He not only was surrogate father to Martha's children Jack and Patsy, but to Jack's two children, Eleanor Custis and George Washington Parke Custis.

19. James Monroe.

20. Martin Van Buren. Ellen Randolph turned him down.

21. William Henry Harrison. One of the two that lived past forty was the father of a later president, Benjamin Harrison.

22. George W. Bush.

23. John Tyler, who had *lots* of kids by his two wives.

24. John F. Kennedy, who in the 1960 campaign flew aboard the *Caroline*.

25. Abraham Lincoln's son Robert, who was present at his father's, and also Garfield's in 1881 and McKinley's in 1901.

✴ 5 ✴

Before They Were Presidents

So Many Lawyers

Do Americans really hate lawyers? If we do, we show it in a funny way: electing them to high office, paying them well, giving them lots of attention, and letting them spend our hard-earned money. Lawyers make up the bulk of political office-holders—yes, including presidents.

1. Who had a reputation as a shrewd, story-telling Illinois lawyer?
2. What Southern lawyer was his state's director of Jimmy Carter's presidential campaign?
3. What wealthy boy passed his bar exam and never bothered finishing law school at Columbia University?
4. Who, as a young lawyer, defended the British soldiers involved in the Boston Massacre?
5. Who, as an Ohio lawyer, helped defend runaway slaves?
6. What poor New York farm boy learned law while clerking for a judge?
7. What Ohio lawyer was made governor of the Philippines by William McKinley?
8. Who, as a New York lawyer, handled a case ruling that blacks could ride the same street cars as whites?
9. Who took night classes at Kansas City Law School but never graduated nor became a lawyer?
10. Who was the first lawyer to become president?
11. Who was admitted to the Virginia bar in 1767?

12. What former president successfully defended the slave mutineers of the ship *Amistad*?

13. Who practiced law in Lancaster, Pennsylvania, before becoming a congressman?

14. Who practiced law in Buffalo, New York, with the firm of Rogers, Bowen, and Rogers?

15. Who, before he became a lawyer, rafted down to New Orleans and worked his way back on a steamer?

16. What Virginian studied law under fellow Virginian Thomas Jefferson?

17. What state capital did Benjamin Harrison serve as city attorney before entering politics?

18. At what prestigious college did the retired Grover Cleveland lecture on law?

19. What hyperactive man studied at Columbia Law School but never became a lawyer?

20. Who gave up his career as a lawyer in Atlanta to go into higher education?

21. Who practiced law in Northampton, Massachusetts, and eventually became the mayor?

22. Who graduated from Duke University's law school and practiced law in California?

23. Who, like most men in his family, was associated with law and politics in Cincinnati?

24. Who practiced law in Grand Rapids, Michigan, before and after serving in World War II?

25. Who studied law at Yale and taught law in Arkansas?

26. Who served as president of the Harvard Law Review?

So Many Lawyers (answers)

1. Abraham Lincoln.
2. Bill Clinton.
3. Franklin Roosevelt.
4. John Adams. Despite his sympathy with the colonists, he did not want to see the soldiers get legally railroaded.
5. Rutherford Hayes.
6. Millard Fillmore.
7. William Howard Taft.
8. Chester Arthur.
9. Harry Truman.
10. John Adams.
11. Thomas Jefferson.
12. John Quincy Adams, who argued the case before the Supreme Court.
13. James Buchanan.
14. Grover Cleveland.
15. Abraham Lincoln.
16. James Monroe.
17. Indianapolis.
18. Princeton.
19. Theodore Roosevelt.
20. Woodrow Wilson.
21. Calvin Coolidge.
22. Richard Nixon.
23. William Howard Taft.
24. Gerald Ford.
25. Bill Clinton.
26. Barack Obama

"No Experience Needed": The Unpolitical Presidents

Life itself is an experience, so, strictly speaking, no president was truly *inexperienced*. Some have, however, gone to the White House as political virgins (more or less).

1. What Mexican War hero had been so nonpolitical that he had never even *voted* for a president?
2. Whose only experience was one term as a congressman and eight years in the Illinois legislature?
3. What popular Union general had served, very briefly, as a stand-in Secretary of War?
4. Who had been sacked from his one political post, collector of the port of New York?
5. What World War II hero had no political background but had been supreme commander of NATO?
6. Whose investments included the Mar-a-Lago private club in Palm Beach and Harrah's in Atlantic City?

"No Experience Needed": The Unpolitical Presidents (answers)

1. Zachary Taylor.
2. Abraham Lincoln.

3. Ulysses S. Grant, who had filled the cabinet post with great reluctance and otherwise had no political experience whatsoever.
4. Chester Arthur. Prior to being elected vice president in 1880, he had never been elected to any office.
5. Dwight Eisenhower. His NATO experience was, no doubt, valuable in his future handling of foreign policy.
6. Donald Trump.

Soldiers into Politicians

Old soldiers never die, they just . . . go into politics. More than a few presidents were military men, some highly successful in both fields, others less so. Rome had Julius Caesar, France had Napoleon, and the U.S. has had . . . well, read on.

1. Whose claim to fame was winning a key battle in the War of 1812—*after* the war had ended? (Hint: hickory)
2. Who served briefly under Zachary Taylor in the Black Hawk War?
3. Who was the only veteran of both the Revolutionary War *and* the French and Indian War?
4. Who made his reputation in the Indian wars, defeating the formidable Tecumseh?
5. What very *unpolitical* career soldier saw action in the War of 1812, the Black Hawk War, and the Mexican War?
6. What frail, tiny man enlisted in a Virginia militia unit but never saw action?
7. In the election of 1852, what Mexican War veteran defeated Mexican War hero Winfield Scott?
8. How many presidents were veterans of the War of 1812?
9. Who served in the army in World War II but was barred from combat because of poor eyesight?
10. Who led a famous charge up San Juan Hill in Cuba?

11. What New Yorker served in the New York state militia during the Civil War?

12. Who dropped out of the College of William and Mary to serve two years in the Continental army?

13. Who joined a dragoon company in the War of 1812, shortly after he became a Pennsylvania lawyer?

14. What Ohio man was chief of staff to Union general William Rosecrans?

15. Who sneaked off from prep school to join in the Spanish-American War?

16. What career soldier chose the date for D-Day in World War II?

17. Who met his future secretary of state, William Rogers, while in naval basic training during World War II?

18. Who was on board *PT-109* when it was rammed by a Japanese destroyer during World War II?

19. Who was drafted in the Civil War but paid $150 to hire a substitute?

20. What World War II navy man was awarded the Distinguished Flying Cross?

21. Who called himself a "plain Hoosier colonel" but was promoted to general in the Civil War?

22. What naval officer was thrown overboard during a typhoon in World War II?

23. What Ohio man took part in fifty Civil War engagements, including the Battle of Antietam?

24. Who served as an officer in the Charles City Rifles in the War of 1812?

25. Who joined the army at age thirteen to fight in the American Revolution?

26. What chunky member of the Twenty-third Ohio Infantry never was wounded or ill during four years of Civil War service?

27. Who held on to his House seat from Texas while serving in World War II as a navy officer?

28. What Southerner is the only president to graduate from the U.S. Naval Academy?

29. What short man proved a flop at business in between successful military stints in the Mexican War and the Civil War?

30. Who served with distinction in France and Germany in World War I?

31. Which two presidents were draft-evaders?

32. Who, while fighting the Creek Indians, had Davy Crockett and Sam Houston among his men?

33. What Southern man with no military experience was given the rank of brigadier general during the Civil War?

34. What Ohio man served as a sergeant under Rutherford Hayes in the Civil War?

35. What navy man, prone to seasickness, carried a bucket with him when he stood watch on ship?

36. Who served in the Texas Air National Guard instead of fighting in Vietnam?

Soldiers into Politicians (answers)

1. Andrew Jackson. Because of slow communications in those days, the Battle of New Orleans, with Jackson as victor, was fought and won after a peace treaty had already been signed.

2. Abraham Lincoln. He admitted he saw no actual fighting during his brief service.

3. George Washington, of course.

4. William Henry Harrison.

5. Zachary Taylor.

6. James Madison.

7. Franklin Pierce.

8. Andrew Jackson, William Henry Harrison, John Tyler, Zachary Taylor, and James Buchanan.

9. Ronald Reagan.

10. Theodore Roosevelt.

11. Chester Arthur.

12. James Monroe.

13. James Buchanan.

14. James Garfield.

15. Franklin Roosevelt. However, sickness prevented him from enlisting.

16. Dwight Eisenhower.

17. Richard Nixon.

18. John F. Kennedy.

19. Grover Cleveland.

20. George H. W. Bush.

21. Benjamin Harrison.

22. Gerald Ford.

23. Rutherford Hayes.

24. John Tyler. Charles City was the name of his home county in Virginia.

25. Andrew Jackson.

26. William McKinley.

27. Lyndon Johnson.

28. Jimmy Carter.

29. Ulysses S. Grant.

30. Harry Truman.
31. Grover Cleveland and Bill Clinton.
32. Andrew Jackson.
33. Andrew Johnson, senator from Tennessee. Because Johnson remained loyal to the Union, Lincoln rewarded him with the post of military governor of occupied Tennessee, which carried the rank (technically) of brigadier general.
34. William McKinley.
35. Jimmy Carter.
36. George W. Bush.

✳ ✳ ✳

Men of the House

The House of Representatives has been, for many, the first step on the Washington ladder, with men going on from there to the Senate or, in some cases, directly to the presidency.

1. Who, as a congressman from California, was a member of the House Un-American Activities Committee?

2. What Virginian was the first House member to move on to the presidency? (Hint: short)

3. What one-term president had a brilliant career in Congress, literally dying in the Capitol?

4. What Tennessean has been the only Speaker of the House to become president?

5. What Union veteran from Ohio almost became Speaker of the House in 1889?

6. What one-term congressman lost in a famous Senate bid but went on to become president?

7. What frontiersman was the first congressman from the new state of Tennessee?

8. What Republican was the only president who had served as minority leader in the House?

9. What Tennessee congressman of several terms got gerry-mandered out of his district? (Hint: tailor)

10. What War of 1812 hero became a congressman from Ohio?

11. What New York congressman helped establish the Whig party in his state?

12. What Democrat from Massachusetts criticized the Truman administration for letting the Communists take China?

13. Who was a supporter of Andrew Jackson in the House before he became a Mexican War soldier?

14. What two Ohioans were still in their Union army uniforms when elected to the House?

15. Who served ten years in the House, first as a Federalist, later as a Democrat?

16. Who served six terms from a Texas district, sometimes running unopposed?

17. Whose long political career included stints as congressman from Virginia, member of the Virginia House of Delegates, *and* member of the Confederate Congress?

18. Who was elected to the House from Texas in 1966, using the campaign slogan "Watch the Action"?

19. Who, in the 1840s, was referred to by a Southern congressman as "the archest enemy of Southern slavery that ever existed"?

Men of the House (answers)

1. Richard Nixon, in the House 1947-50.

2. James Madison, who was congressman from Virginia 1789-97.

3. John Quincy Adams, who collapsed from a stroke on the House floor on February 21, 1848, and died two days later.

4. James K. Polk, member of the House 1825-39, Speaker of the House 1835-39.

5. William McKinley, who served in the House 1877-83 and 1885-91.

6. Abraham Lincoln, who served in the House 1848-49, but lost his famous Senate race against Stephen Douglas. He had the pleasure of beating Douglas in the 1860 presidential election.

7. Andrew Jackson, who served 1797-98.

8. Gerald Ford, who held the post 1965-73.

9. Andrew Johnson, who dealt with the situation by successfully running for governor.

10. William Henry Harrison.

11. Millard Fillmore, who went on to become a Whig vice president and then president.

12. John F. Kennedy, in the House 1947-53.

13. Franklin Pierce.

14. Rutherford Hayes and James Garfield.

15. James Buchanan.

16. Lyndon Johnson.

17. John Tyler, who died before actually taking his seat in the Confederate Congress.

18. George H. W. Bush, who served 1967-71.

19. John Quincy Adams, who, in his long House career, was a thorn in the side of pro-slavery men.

States' Men: Governors into Presidents

More than a few presidents were ex-governors, and some say it is a logical leap to go from chief executive from a state to chief executive of a nation. Whether the former governors were competent and whether they made good presidents is open to debate.

1. Who served two years as governor of Virginia during the Revolutionary War?

2. What Barry Goldwater supporter served two terms as governor of California?

3. Who, while governor of Georgia, headed the Democratic National Committee?

4. Who delivered "fireside chats" via radio while governor of New York?

5. Who ran against popular Democrat Ann Richards for Texas governor and won?

6. Who went from being president of Princeton University to governor of New Jersey?

7. Who was serving his second term as Ohio governor when nominated for the presidency?

8. Who became governor of New York with the aid of political boss Thomas Platt?

9. What former *elected* governor of Tennessee was made *military* governor of Tennessee during wartime?

10. Who, in one term as governor of Virginia, put down a slave revolt?

11. Who was made governor of the Indiana Territory by John Adams?

12. Who served as military governor of Florida after fighting the Seminoles there?

13. Who served one term as Tennessee governor before running for president three years later?

14. Who served as governor of New York for only two months in 1829?

15. Who, in 1827, resigned his post as Virginia governor to become a senator?

16. What Ohio governor called out the National Guard to put down a labor dispute?

17. What Vermont native gained fame as Massachusetts governor by putting down a police strike?

18. Who was defeated in a run for California governor *after* being defeated as a presidential candidate?

19. Who is the only president who was governor of Arkansas?

20. Which state has had the most governors go on to become president?

21. Which former president had two sons serving as governors in two different states?

22. What New York governor had the slogan "Public office is a public trust"?

23. What notable Virginia orator did Thomas Jefferson succeed as governor of Virginia?

24. Who, while serving as Tennessee's governor, made a suit of clothes for the governor of Kentucky?

25. What reform-minded New York governor stood up to the corrupt Tammany Hall political machine?

States' Men: Governors into Presidents (answers)

1. Thomas Jefferson. He did not consider it the high point of his brilliant career.
2. Ronald Reagan.
3. Jimmy Carter.
4. Franklin Roosevelt.
5. George W. Bush. Richards accused him of being "born with a silver foot in his mouth."
6. Woodrow Wilson.
7. Rutherford Hayes.
8. Theodore Roosevelt, who, to Platt's dismay, did not follow all his advice afterward.
9. Andrew Johnson. He was the only Southern senator who remained in D.C. when his state seceded, so his loyalty was rewarded with the post of military governor.
10. James Monroe.
11. William Henry Harrison.
12. Andrew Jackson.
13. James K. Polk.
14. Martin Van Buren. He left to assume the office of Secretary of State under Andrew Jackson.
15. John Tyler.
16. William McKinley.
17. Calvin Coolidge.
18. Richard Nixon. He did return, of course.
19. Bill Clinton.
20. New York: Martin Van Buren, Grover Cleveland, Theodore Roosevelt, and Franklin Roosevelt.
21. George H. W. Bush, father of Jeb Bush (Florida) and George W. Bush (Texas).

22. Grover Cleveland.
23. Patrick Henry, of "Give me liberty or give me death" fame.
24. Andrew Johnson, who was a tailor by trade and never became too uppity to ply his needle.
25. Grover Cleveland.

From Mr. Secretary to Mr. Prez

Being an advisor to a president doesn't necessarily make one presidential material. Even so, a few cabinet members have gone on to the presidency. Some of these you know about, and some may really surprise you.

1. From what cabinet post have the most presidents "graduated"?
2. Who was the first president to have been a cabinet member?
3. Who was the only 20th-century Secretary of War to become president?
4. And who was the only Secretary of Commerce to become president? (Hint: the Depression)
5. What Virginia protégé of Jefferson served as his Secretary of State for eight years?
6. Who, as Secretary of State, supported President Polk's annexation of Texas? (Hint: unmarried)
7. What wealthy New York man was Assistant Secretary of the Navy 1913-20?
8. What fellow Virginian was James Madison's Secretary of State for eight years?
9. Who was newly elected governor of New York but left after two months to be Andrew Jackson's Secretary of State?
10. What New England man went from being ambassador to Great Britain to being Secretary of State?
11. Who was the only president who had held two cabinet posts *simultaneously*?

12. What plum post did Theodore Roosevelt offer Taft before Taft accepted the post of Secretary of War?

13. What man, while Commerce Secretary, reduced the working day from twelve hours to the now standard eight?

From Mr. Secretary to Mr. Prez (answers)

1. Secretary of State. There have been six who became president: Jefferson, Madison, Monroe, J. Q. Adams, Van Buren, and James Buchanan.

2. Thomas Jefferson, who was Secretary of State for George Washington.

3. William Howard Taft, who held the post under Theodore Roosevelt.

4. Herbert Hoover, who held the post under Coolidge.

5. James Madison.

6. James Buchanan.

7. Franklin Roosevelt.

8. James Monroe.

9. Martin Van Buren.

10. John Quincy Adams, appointed to the cabinet by James Monroe.

11. James Monroe. He was Madison's Secretary of State 1811-17, and also Secretary of War 1814-15.

12. Supreme Court justice. Years later, Taft accepted the post of chief justice from Warren Harding.

13. Herbert Hoover.

✻   ✻   ✻

Senators Who Got Promoted

With 100 members today, the Senate is considered a highly exclusive political club, and it was even more so when its members were fewer. Entire books have been written on the senators who became president, as well as the many who tried but failed.

1. What Massachusetts senator's family was close to controversial Senator Joe McCarthy?

2. What Southern man served in the Senate both before and after his presidency? (Hint: impeach)

3. Who was a senator from the newly created state of Tennessee?

4. What Californian campaigned for the Senate with "pink sheets," trying to paint his opponent as pro-Communist?

5. What Indiana lawyer's only elected office before the presidency was that of senator?

6. Who went from serving in the New York Senate to the U.S. Senate?

7. What senator was rewarded for supporting James K. Polk by being made Secretary of State?

8. What Ohio man, who loved his whiskey, voted *for* Prohibition while a senator?

9. Who was criticized while senator for his ties to a Kansas City political boss?

10. What War of 1812 veteran was a senator from Ohio?

11. What Virginia native was the first senator to make it to the presidency?

12. In the 1820s, who went from being governor of Virginia to senator?

13. What New Englander became a senator in 1836 at age 32?

14. What Texan changed, in his Senate years, his attitude toward civil rights legislation?

15. Who is the only Illinois senator to become president?

Senators Who Got Promoted (answers)

1. John F. Kennedy's. His brother Robert had served on McCarthy's staff.
2. Andrew Johnson, who was the only ex-president to serve in the Senate.
3. Andrew Jackson, senator 1797-98 (he resigned after only five months), and again 1823-25 (he resigned again).
4. Richard Nixon. The sheets worked, for Nixon won against the very liberal incumbent.
5. Benjamin Harrison.
6. Martin Van Buren, U.S. senator 1821-28.
7. James Buchanan.
8. Warren Harding.
9. Harry Truman, a protégé of boss Thomas Pendergast.
10. William Henry Harrison, senator 1825-28.
11. James Monroe, senator from Virginia 1790-94.
12. John Tyler.
13. Franklin Pierce.
14. Lyndon Johnson.
15. Barack Obama.

✴   ✴   ✴

It's a Living

Most of our presidents weren't *born* into politics and (with a few exceptions) most had to make a living, at least in their younger years. See how much you know about the various ways they made ends meet in their pre-presidential years.

1. Whose acting co-stars included Ann Sheridan, Pat O'Brien, and a chimp named Bonzo?

2. Who, as a New York City employee, walked the streets trying to catch policemen goofing off?

3. Who, in his younger days, formed a company known as the Adventurers for Draining the Great Dismal Swamp?

4. Who had no formal education but made his living as a tailor?

5. Who made himself a millionaire through his work as a mining engineer?

6. What future military hero eked out a meager living selling firewood in St. Louis?

7. Who was the only newspaper publisher to become president?

8. What very successful soldier and unsuccessful president failed at every other job he held, including farming?

9. Who was mayor of Buffalo, then governor of New York?

10. Who was a lay preacher, college professor, college president, and Union officer?

11. What dyslexic man was a political science professor and college president?

12. Who left his posh life in Connecticut to work in the Texas oil business?

13. What city boy briefly ran a cattle-herding business near the Maltese Cross Ranch?

14. What Republican in his younger days was a barker for the Wheel of Chance at a rodeo?

15. What athletic Michigan man was a model for *Look* magazine?
16. Who left his navy job to run his family's peanut business?
17. Whose jobs included postal clerk, Union soldier, and Ohio lawyer?
18. Who failed at running his Kansas City clothing store?
19. Who graduated from a Texas teachers' college and had a very brief teaching career before entering politics?
20. What New Yorker referred to businessmen as "flubdubs" and "mollycoddles"?

It's a Living (answers)

1. Ronald Reagan.
2. Theodore Roosevelt, who as police commissioner was determined to clean up a lazy, corrupt force.
3. George Washington. The Dismal Swamp is on the Virginia-Carolina border, mostly in Virginia.
4. The "Tennessee Tailor," Andrew Johnson.
5. Herbert Hoover, a more successful engineer than president.
6. Ulysses S. Grant.
7. Warren Harding.
8. Ulysses S. Grant.
9. Grover Cleveland.

10. James Garfield.
11. Woodrow Wilson, president of Princeton.
12. George H. W. Bush.
13. Theodore Roosevelt.
14. Richard Nixon.
15. Gerald Ford.
16. Jimmy Carter.
17. William McKinley.
18. Harry Truman.
19. Lyndon Johnson.
20. Theodore Roosevelt.

Whose Colorful Career Was This?

Here's a quickie test: three items from the career of each president. Then name the man.

1. U.S. Naval Academy midshipman; Georgia legislator; governor of Georgia

2. navy pilot in World War II; oil company manager; UN ambassador

3. California lawyer; World War II naval officer; senator from California

4. Missouri farmer; World War I army officer; county judge

5. farmer; major in Virginia militia; president of Constitutional Convention

6. tailor; mayor of Greeneville, Tennessee; governor of Tennessee

7. Harvard Business School student; Air National Guard pilot; governor of Texas

8. graduated from Harvard; author of the Massachusetts constitution; U.S. diplomat in Europe

9. U.S. Civil Service Commission; Spanish-American War officer; governor of New York

10. high school teacher; congressman from Texas; naval officer in World War II

11. Eureka College graduate; actor; governor of California

12. graduate of the College of William and Mary; ambassador to France; Secretary of State under Washington

13. lawyer in North Carolina; congressman from Tennessee; general in War of 1812

14. U.S. Military Academy cadet; commander of tank training school; aide to General Douglas MacArthur

15. football star at University of Michigan; Yale Law School student; House Minority Leader

16. New York lawyer; New York legislator; governor of New York

17. Yale graduate; U.S. circuit judge; governor of the Philippines

18. Illinois legislator; congressman; lawyer

19. governor of Virginia; senator from Virginia; Confederate congressman

20. Virginia legislature; Constitutional Convention delegate; wrote some of *The Federalist Papers*

21. Bowdoin College graduate; congressman from New Hampshire; Mexican War general

22. country school teacher; Union army officer; governor of Ohio

23. Stanford graduate; mining engineer in China; United States Food Administrator

24. college president; Ohio legislator; Union army general

25. governor of Virginia; negotiator of Louisiana Purchase; Secretary of State

26. U.S. army officer; Mexican War hero; plantation owner

27. sheriff of Erie County, New York; mayor of Buffalo; governor of New York

28. Massachusetts lawyer; president of Massachusetts Senate; governor of Massachusetts

29. attended Stanford business school; navy officer in World War II; senator from Massachusetts

30. senator from Massachusetts; Secretary of State; congressman from Massachusetts

31. Yale Law School graduate; attorney general of Arkansas; governor of Arkansas

32. attended University of Virginia law school; professor at Bryn Mawr College; governor of New Jersey

33. attorney general of New York; Secretary of State; ambassador to England

34. lawyer in New York state; Whig congressman; chairman of Ways and Means Committee

35. Union College graduate; lawyer in New York City; collector of the port of New York

36. governor of Indiana Territory; War of 1812 general; ambassador to Colombia

37. lawyer in Tennessee; Speaker of the House; governor of Tennessee

38. Dickinson College graduate; Pennsylvania legislator; ambassador to Russia

39. U.S. army officer; Missouri farmer; Illinois store clerk

40. Miami University graduate; Indianapolis lawyer; senator from Indiana

41. studied law at Harvard; Ohio lawyer; governor of Ohio

42. Harvard Law Review president, community organizer, Illinois senator

43. newspaper publisher; Ohio legislator; senator from Ohio

44. reality TV host, casino owner, Fordham student

Whose Colorful Career Was This? (answers)

1. Jimmy Carter.
2. George H. W. Bush.
3. Richard Nixon.
4. Harry Truman.
5. George Washington.
6. Andrew Johnson.
7. George W. Bush.
8. John Adams.
9. Theodore Roosevelt.
10. Lyndon Johnson.
11. Ronald Reagan.
12. Thomas Jefferson.
13. Andrew Jackson.
14. Dwight Eisenhower.
15. Gerald Ford.
16. Franklin Roosevelt.
17. William Howard Taft.
18. Abraham Lincoln.
19. John Tyler.
20. James Madison.
21. Franklin Pierce.
22. William McKinley.
23. Herbert Hoover.
24. James Garfield.
25. James Monroe.
26. Zachary Taylor.
27. Grover Cleveland.
28. Calvin Coolidge.
29. John F. Kennedy.
30. John Quincy Adams.

31. Bill Clinton.
32. Woodrow Wilson.
33. Martin Van Buren.
34. Millard Fillmore.
35. Chester Arthur.
36. William Henry Harrison.
37. James K. Polk.
38. James Buchanan.
39. Ulysses S. Grant.
40. Benjamin Harrison.
41. Rutherford Hayes.
42. Barack Obama.
43. Warren Harding.
44. Donald Trump

✶ ✶ ✶

At Loose and Abroad: Foreign Service

Quite a few presidents never set foot outside the U.S., but quite a few did, sometimes as diplomats. No one doubts that foreign experience is great background for handling foreign affairs while president.

1. Who was ambassador to China, 1974-75?
2. What Virginian was America's first ambassador to France?
3. What mining engineer gained worldwide fame during World War I by providing relief to war-ravaged Europe?
4. Who was governor-general of the Philippines? (Hint: chunky)
5. What pudgy man was ambassador to both Russia and to Great Britain, with a cabinet stint in between the two?
6. What son of an ambassador was himself ambassador to the Netherlands, to Prussia, to Russia, and to Great Britain?
7. What Virginian was ambassador to France in the 1790s and never got over his love affair with the country? (Hint: no, not Jefferson)

8. Who was a member of a three-man commission to France from 1778 to 1788?

9. Who took a break from college to serve as secretary to his father, the ambassador to Great Britain?

At Loose and Abroad: Foreign Service (answers)

1. George H. W. Bush. His actual title was "Chief U.S. Liaison in China," since (technically) there was no actual ambassador at the time.

2. Thomas Jefferson. By the way, for many years U.S. diplomats were called "ministers" instead of "ambassadors."

3. Herbert Hoover.

4. William Howard Taft.

5. James Buchanan.

6. John Quincy Adams, whose father John had also held posts abroad.

7. James Monroe.

8. John Adams.

9. John F. Kennedy.

While They Were Vice Presidents

Several of our presidents have died in office, elevating Number Two Man to Number One in a hurry. And there were other vice presidents who were elected in their own right. While it hasn't proved to be *the* stepping stone to the White House, the vice presidency has provided us with more than a few presidents, and some of their vice-presidential careers were quite colorful.

1. Who, appropriately, was the first president who had been vice president?
2. What plain-spoken Democrat described his vice presidency as "about as useful as a cow's fifth teat"?
3. Who was awakened from a sound sleep to be told that a bullet had made him president?
4. What reform-minded New Yorker was forced on the Republican ticket by political bosses who wanted him out of New York?
5. Who, as a vice-presidential candidate under fire, delivered his famous "Checkers" speech on TV?
6. Who served as "acting president" for eight hours while the Republican president underwent cancer surgery?
7. What intellectual spent his off-hours as vice president by writing *A Manual of Parliamentary Practice*? (Hint: Virginia)
8. What tight-lipped redhead had the presidential oath of office administered at his family home by his own father?
9. What Virginian had the shortest vice-presidency?
10. What New Yorker was the first vice-presidential candidate handpicked by the presidential candidate?
11. What Northerner never met his presidential running mate, a Southerner, until after they were elected?
12. Who, a vice president for only seven months, had never held any elected office?

13. Who, as vice president, served as chairman of the National Aeronautics and Space Council?

14. Who was never elected to either the presidency or the vice presidency?

15. Who was the only vice president to run on the Union ticket?

16. Who stumped the country making 673 speeches while his presidential running mate remained at home?

17. What vice president lost his first presidential bid but won eight years later?

18. What Democrat was elected vice president in the same election in which he ran for senator from Texas?

While They Were Vice Presidents (answers)

1. John Adams, of course. He did not have a high opinion of his position.

2. Harry Truman, who had slightly over a month in the office before FDR died.

3. Andrew Johnson, who became president after Lincoln's assassination. Johnson himself was one of the targets in the assassination plot.

4. Theodore Roosevelt. The bosses had no idea that, because of McKinley's assassination, the former governor would become president.

5. Richard Nixon.

6. George H. W. Bush. This was on July 13, 1985.

7. Thomas Jefferson. The manual is still used in the Senate.

8. Calvin Coolidge, who was staying with his father when Warren Harding died. His father was both a justice of the peace and a notary, so he was qualified to administer the oath.

9. John Tyler, since William Henry Harrison died after only a month in office.

10. Martin Van Buren, the friend and protégé of Andrew Jackson, who succeeded in his wish that Van Buren be his successor.

11. Millard Fillmore, who never met Zachary Taylor during the campaign.

12. Chester Arthur, who became president after the assassination of James Garfield.

13. Lyndon Johnson.

14. Gerald Ford, who was *appointed* vice president by Nixon after Spiro Agnew resigned, then became president when Nixon himself resigned.

15. Andrew Johnson. In the 1864 election the Republican party renamed itself for that one election only. Johnson himself had been a lifelong Democrat.

16. Theodore Roosevelt. William McKinley, considered a shoo-in for a second term, did not campaign.

17. Richard Nixon.

18. Lyndon Johnson, who ran for both offices in 1960.

Educating the Presidents

Education-wise, our presidents make up a motley crew—from zero schooling to multiple graduate degrees, and everything in between. Worth noting: While we've had a few unschooled presidents, we've had no *uneducated* ones. A few of our chief executives were largely self-educated, but no less intelligent for that. Also worth noting: Some of our must successful and admired presidents were among those with the least formal schooling. Hmmm.

1. Who majored in economics at Eureka College in Illinois?

2. Who followed up his World War II pilot service by completing his Yale education in two-and-a-half years?

3. What Virginia-born man was the only president with an earned doctoral degree?

4. What wise Virginian studied two years at the College of William and Mary before serving a five-year law apprenticeship?

5. What future general was 5'1" when he entered West Point, just barely meeting the academy's height requirement?

6. What New Englander had by age 18 mastered Latin, Greek, French, Dutch, and Spanish?

7. Who was taught to read while working as an apprentice tailor?

8. What Virginian graduated from the College of William and Mary at age 17 and studied law under his father?

9. What successful lawyer and voracious reader estimated that he had had about one year of schooling? (Hint: tall)

10. Who became bosom buddies with Nathaniel Hawthorne while they were students at Bowdoin College in Maine?

11. Who was born in North Carolina, grew up in Tennessee, and returned to be educated at the University of North Carolina?

12. What self-taught man enrolled in an academy at age 19 and eventually married his teacher? (Hint: New York)

13. Who was nearly booted out of Pennsylvania's Dickinson College for his pranks?

14. Who, unlike his older brothers, was schooled in Virginia instead of England? (Hint: early)

15. What minister's son turned down an offer to have his college education paid for if he would become a minister?

16. What grandson of a president graduated from Miami University of Ohio?

17. What sickly New York boy studied under private tutors until he entered Harvard in 1876?

18. Who was teased unmercifully at the Naval Academy for his Southern accent?

19. Who never attended college but did attend Kansas City Law School?

20. Who majored in history at Whittier College, where he was captain of the debating team?

21. Who launched his long career in newspaper publishing by starting a campus paper at Ohio Central College?

22. What sizable man attended Yale and the University of Cincinnati Law School?

23. What Nebraska-born man went to the University of Michigan where he played football?

24. What New York man was the only president to graduate from Union College in Schenectady?

25. Who was the only president to attend both Princeton and Harvard?

26. Who was educated by private tutors, including teachers of dance, drawing, and piano?

27. Who worked his way through an Illinois college by acting as a lifeguard and by washing dishes in his fraternity house?

28. Whose education included time at Georgia Tech and at the U.S. Naval Academy?

29. What future military leader chose West Point because the Naval Academy rejected him as being too old?

30. Who worked his way through Southwest Texas State Teachers College by collecting trash and janitoring?

Educating the Presidents (answers)

1. Ronald Reagan.
2. George H. W. Bush.
3. Woodrow Wilson, with a Ph.D. in political science from Johns Hopkins University.
4. Thomas Jefferson.
5. Ulysses S. Grant.
6. John Quincy Adams.
7. Andrew Johnson. An old story was that his wife taught him to read, but in fact he already knew how to read when he married her.
8. John Tyler.
9. Abraham Lincoln.
10. Franklin Pierce.
11. James K. Polk.
12. Millard Fillmore.
13. James Buchanan.
14. George Washington.
15. Grover Cleveland, who instead became a lawyer.
16. Benjamin Harrison.
17. Theodore Roosevelt.
18. Jimmy Carter.
19. Harry S. Truman.
20. Richard Nixon.
21. Warren Harding.
22. William Howard Taft.
23. Gerald Ford.
24. Chester A. Arthur.
25. John F. Kennedy, who left Princeton due to health problems.
26. Franklin Roosevelt.

27. Ronald Reagan.
28. Jimmy Carter.
29. Dwight Eisenhower.
30. Lyndon Johnson.

What School Graduated Us?

Try this: read the list of names in each question and match the names with the college that graduated them all.

1. Dwight Eisenhower, Ulysses S. Grant
2. John Adams, John Quincy Adams, Theodore Roosevelt
3. Bill Clinton, George W. Bush
4. Thomas Jefferson, James Monroe, John Tyler
5. Franklin Pierce
6. James Madison, Woodrow Wilson
7. Herbert Hoover
8. William Henry Harrison
9. William Howard Taft, Gerald Ford, George H. W. Bush
10. James K. Polk
11. James Garfield
12. James Buchanan
13. Rutherford Hayes
14. Chester Arthur
15. Benjamin Harrison
16. Calvin Coolidge
17. Franklin Roosevelt, John F. Kennedy, Barack Obama
18. Jimmy Carter

What School Graduated Us? (answers)

1. U.S. Military Academy (West Point).
2. Harvard.
3. Yale.
4. College of William and Mary, Virginia.
5. Bowdoin College, Maine.
6. Princeton (known as the College of New Jersey in the old days).
7. Stanford University.
8. Hampden-Sydney College, Virginia.
9. Yale, again.
10. University of North Carolina.
11. Williams College, Massachusetts.
12. Dickinson College, Pennsylvania.
13. Kenyon College, Ohio.
14. Union College, New York.
15. Miami University, Ohio.
16. Amherst College, Massachusetts.
17. Harvard, again.
18. U.S. Naval Academy.

Educating the Presidents (Part 2)

1. What tight-lipped New Englander graduated from Amherst College in Massachusetts?
2. What Virginian graduated from Princeton but stayed on an extra year to study Hebrew and philosophy?
3. Who studied at the London School of Economics in 1935?
4. Who was known as "Gloomy Gus" while a student at Duke University Law School? (Hint: the nose)
5. Who dropped out of high school but was among the first

class at the new Stanford University?

6. Who studied law at Georgetown University in the 1930s but never took a degree?

7. Who was kept out of West Point and the Naval Academy by his poor eyesight?

8. Who took off time from Harvard to serve as an aide to his father, the ambassador to Britain?

9. Who continued his Harvard education an extra year because he enjoyed editing the college newspaper?

10. What much-educated president attended Davidson, Princeton, the University of Virginia, and Johns Hopkins?

11. What Ohio man attended Allegheny College and Albany Law School but never took a degree?

12. Who was the only president with a degree in geology?

13. What extremely large man took dancing lessons while in high school?

14. Whose hobbies while at Harvard included birdwatching and boxing?

15. What Civil War veteran was 1842 class valedictorian of Kenyon College of Ohio?

16. What future military leader was horrified to learn his father had arranged his appointment to West Point?

17. Which president did not attend a single day of school?

18. What Virginian was the only president to attend Hampden-Sydney College?

19. Who attended Occidental College in California before transferring to Columbia?

20. What New Englander received his childhood education at a Paris academy, a Dutch university, and Harvard?

21. Who dropped out of the College of William and Mary, fought in the Revolution, and studied law under Thomas Jefferson?

22. Who coached football while attending Yale Law School?

23. What future political whiz was educated at the Kinderhook Academy in New York?

24. What Massachusetts boy was sent to Harvard by his farmer father in hopes he would be a minister?

25. Who worked for the family business while pursuing his degree in economics?

26. What president, receiving an honorary doctorate from Harvard, caused alumnus John Quincy Adams to gripe?

Educating the Presidents (Part 2) (answers)

1. Calvin Coolidge.
2. James Madison. At that time Princeton was called the College of New Jersey.
3. John F. Kennedy.
4. Richard Nixon.
5. Herbert Hoover.
6. Lyndon Johnson.
7. Harry S. Truman.
8. John F. Kennedy.
9. Franklin Roosevelt, editor of the Harvard *Crimson.*
10. Woodrow Wilson.
11. William McKinley.

12. Herbert Hoover, a Stanford alumnus.
13. William Howard Taft.
14. Theodore Roosevelt.
15. Rutherford Hayes.
16. Ulysses S. Grant, who at the time had no plans for a military life.
17. Andrew Johnson, probably a classic example of a self-made man.
18. William Henry Harrison.
19. Barack Obama.
20. John Quincy Adams.
21. James Monroe.
22. Gerald Ford.
23. Martin Van Buren, "Old Kinderhook" himself.
24. John Adams, who instead became a lawyer.
25. Donald Trump.
26. Andrew Jackson. Adams muttered that Jackson could barely write his name.

CHAPTER

✳ 6 ✳

The Man in Private

Booze and Tobacco—Pleasure and Pain

Not many of our presidents were teetotalers, and quite of few of them were tobacco users (quite common in the days before Surgeon General warnings). The use of alcohol ranged from absolute zero to occasional drinkers to serious alcoholics. Where tobacco is concerned, some presidents enjoyed an occasional puff, while others died from the long-term effects.

1. Who vowed in 1789 that henceforth he would only drink beer made in America?

2. What Ohio man voted for Prohibition while he was a senator, then kept bootleg liquor at the White House?

3. What chubby New Englander began smoking at age eight?

4. Who got a reputation as a drunk after appearing intoxicated at Lincoln's inauguration?

5. What Virginia man ran up a $10,000 wine bill while president?

6. Who, of all the presidents, was the most notorious smoker? (Hint: military man)

7. What quiet man abstained from drinking, but only while Prohibition was on?

8. What tall Texan smoked three packs a day but quit after a heart attack?

9. Which Virginian was sold to voters as a simple "hard cider" drinker?

10. What frontiersman kept a large pipe collection but preferred smoking his own simple corncob pipe?

11. What non-drinking, non-smoking president was married to the non-drinking "Lemonade Lucy"?

12. What sophisticated Democrat liked his martinis and his "Haitian libation," a cocktail made with rum and brown sugar?

13. What religious man was urged by temperance groups to be a teetotaler but refused?

14. What handsome president was an alcoholic, as was his mother?

15. What physical fitness fanatic never smoked and hardly ever drank?

16. What portly man loved his cigars and was known to frequent the beer gardens in Buffalo, New York?

17. Who, in the Prohibition era, would drink at the Belgian embassy?

18. What very religious Ohio man played cards, smoked cigars, and drank scotch in the White House?

19. What military man neither smoked nor drank but loved to chew tobacco?

20. What nonsmoking Baptist Democrat liked his white wine and bourbon?

21. Who was notorious for smoking his cigarettes in a holder?

22. Who began rolling his own cigarettes at West Point, eventually leading to a habit of four packs a day?

23. What European-reared president was a wine connoisseur?

24. Who was sometimes photographed with a pipe in his younger days but in fact never smoked?

25. What 21st-century president claimed he was trying to give up cigarettes?

26. What clean-living man loved cigars but refused to be photographed with one?

27. Whose candidacy was in peril because it was revealed a few days before the election that he had a DUI conviction?

Booze and Tobacco—Pleasure and Pain (answers)

1. George Washington. Specifically, he referred to *porter*, a type of ale, browner and creamier than most beers of today.

2. Warren Harding. During his administration, the White House was probably at its booziest and smokiest.

3. John Adams.

4. Andrew Johnson's, the vice president. In fact, Johnson didn't drink much, but his behavior at the inauguration was never forgotten.

5. Thomas Jefferson.

6. Undoubtedly Ulysses S. Grant, who smoked about 20 cigars a day, which no doubt led to the cancer that eventually killed him.

7. Calvin Coolidge. He was not a teetotaler, but, unlike his predecessor Warren Harding, he wasn't willing to drink when it was illegal.

8. Lyndon Johnson.

9. William Henry Harrison, who ran, successfully, his "hard cider" campaign against Martin Van Buren who was presented as an effete wine-drinker (which he was).

10. Andrew Jackson.

11. Rutherford Hayes, whose wife Lucy banned alcohol from all state functions at the White House.

12. Franklin Roosevelt.

13. James A. Garfield. Perhaps the temperance groups were pleased that in the previous administration (Rutherford Hayes's) the White House was "dry," and they hoped Garfield would continue that habit.

14. Franklin Pierce.

15. Theodore Roosevelt.

16. Grover Cleveland.

17. Herbert Hoover. Technically, he wasn't breaking the law since embassies are foreign soil, so he was "out of the country" while boozing at the embassy.

18. William McKinley.

19. Zachary Taylor. His aim at a spittoon was, they said, remarkable.

20. Harry S. Truman. (He did not, by the way, like white wine and bourbon *together*.)

21. Franklin Roosevelt, who smoked a pack a day.

22. Dwight Eisenhower.

23. John Quincy Adams.

24. Ronald Reagan.

25. Barack Obama.

26. William McKinley, again. He feared it would set a bad example for the young.

27. George W. Bush, in the 2000 election.

The Presidential Look

Looks aren't everything, and in the pre-TV age the country could stomach such unattractive presidents as Abraham Lincoln and John Quincy Adams. (Of course, in the TV era we managed to tolerate Lyndon Johnson, didn't we?) Still, every good politician knows that image counts, and even a chubby, unattractive man like John Adams understood the importance of dressing well on public occasions. Truth is, our presidents' looks fascinate us, from the familiar Gilbert Stuart image of Washington to photographs of the homely Lincoln to Richard Nixon's ski-slope nose to . . .

1. Who (as if you couldn't guess) was the first president to wear false teeth?

2. What Democrat's trademark was his gray, brushed-up hairstyle?

3. Who was the first president to wear a beard? (Hint: penny)

4. What Tennessean's occupation insured he was always well-dressed?

5. What portly New Englander talked with a lisp because he refused to wear his dentures?

6. What 20th-century Republican was both right- and left-handed?

7. What scrawny New York boy turned into the brawny president remembered for his toothy grin and bushy mustache?

8. What tall, sandy-haired Virginian always impressed visitors as *extremely* casual in his look?

9. Who, at 6'1" and 140 pounds, would definitely qualify as the thinnest president? (Hint: War of 1812 hero)

10. Who, nicknamed "Big Lub," was 332 pounds at one point?

11. Who, though considered one of the most handsome presidents ever, wore corrective shoes because one leg was shorter than the other?

12. What tiny man weighed in at barely a hundred pounds and had a nose scarred by frostbite?

13. What one-term president was best-known for his curly dark hair?

14. What Virginian was the last president to wear knee britches?

15. What pudgy Dutchman was noted for having no facial hair but prominent gray side whiskers?

16. Who made a grin and a long cigarette holder part of his public look?

17. What one-termer was noted for "wryneck," always cocking his head to one side?

18. What short, bearded man was only 5'1" when he entered West Point?

19. Whose neck was so thick that people joked he could take his shirt off without unbuttoning the collar?

20. Who always liked to wear a carnation for good luck?

21. What philandering man was noted for his heavy black eyebrows and silvery hair?

22. Who, by most people's standards, was the ugliest president?

23. What Union veteran was caricatured for his shortness, his paunch, and his spindly legs?

24. What Republican, a former magazine model, also boasted that he was "the most athletic president to occupy the White House in years"?

25. What recent president insisted that, despite his age, he did *not* color the gray out of his hair?

26. What thin redhead slicked his hair down with Vaseline?

27. What retired general is remembered for his baldness, big ears, and extremely wide smile?

28. What dapper gent wore sidewhiskers and a mustache, and changed clothes several times each day?

29. What Republican is remembered not only for his jowls but for his distinctive "ski slope" nose?

30. What minister's son was noted for his "professorish" look?

31. Who, noted for his toothy grin, was the first 20th-century president to have hair touching his ears?

32. Who got his "slovenly" nickname from his total carelessness about his appearance?

33. Who, after being elected, grew a beard at the suggestion of a young girl?

34. What 20th-century Republican had such a heavy beard that he had to shave two or three times a day?

The Presidential Look (answers)

1. George Washington. But they were *not* made of wood.

2. Bill Clinton. Rumor has it that he had it dyed gray so as to look more "presidential."

3. Abraham Lincoln, of course.

4. Andrew Johnson. Although he came from a poor background, he was a tailor, and so managed to dress nicely.

5. "His Rotundity," John Adams.

6. Gerald Ford, who performed some tasks with one hand, some with the other.

7. Theodore Roosevelt.

8. Thomas Jefferson.

9. Andrew Jackson.

10. William Howard Taft, remembered for getting stuck in the White House bathtub.

11. John F. Kennedy.

12. James Madison.

13. Franklin Pierce, "Handsome Frank," better to look at than to govern.

14. James Monroe. By the time of his presidency, knee britches were already "out," but Monroe was old-fashioned.

15. Martin Van Buren.

16. Franklin Roosevelt.

17. James Buchanan, who always cocked his head to the left.

18. Ulysses S. Grant.

19. Grover Cleveland.

20. William McKinley.

21. Warren Harding, who (so it was said) got the women's vote in the first election when they *could* vote.

22. Some would say Lyndon Johnson, but most people would agree on Abraham Lincoln. With his huge ears, sallow skin, prominent wart, heavy eyebrows, and lankiness, Lincoln admitted he was no beauty.

23. Benjamin Harrison.

24. Gerald Ford. He was probably right, yet he is remembered for several times falling down in public.

25. Ronald Reagan.

26. Calvin Coolidge.

27. Dwight Eisenhower.

28. Chester Arthur, known as "Elegant Arthur," "The Dude President," etc.

29. Richard Nixon.

30. Woodrow Wilson.

31. Jimmy Carter. In fact, he was the *only* 20th-century president whose hair touched his ears.

32. Zachary Taylor, "Old Rough and Ready."

33. Abraham Lincoln. On his way to Washington, Lincoln met with the little girl who had offered the suggestion and gave her a kiss.

34. Richard Nixon.

Things of the Spirit

"Separation of church and state" is *not* (contrary to popular belief) mentioned in the Constitution at all, but even if it were, all the presidents have been willing to pay lip service to the importance of faith in God. In some cases it was *just* lip service, for wise politicians know that Americans like their presidents to at least *seem* religious. But more than a few presidents were in fact deeply religious men, and quite a few of them knew the Bible well.

1. What Baptist proclaimed the first annual day of prayer? (Hint: plain-spoken)

2. What early president spoke of the Bible as "the Rock on which our Republic rests"? (Hint: general and Indian fighter)

3. What intellectual Virginian "edited" the Gospels, cutting out all the supernatural elements?

4. What Presbyterian pastor's son claimed that "My life would not be worth living if it were not for the driving power of religion"?

5. What born-again Baptist had a sister who was an evangelist and healer?

6. What extremely devout Methodist invited guests to "hymn sings" on Sunday in the White House Blue Room? (Hint: assassinated)

7. Who rejected his Quaker parents' pacifism and enlisted in the navy in World War II?

8. What Democrat claimed he disliked the D.C. tourists watching him during church services?

9. What assassinated president had served for a time as a Disciples of Christ evangelist?

10. What Unitarian from Massachusetts recited the familiar prayer "Now I lay me down to sleep" every night?

11. What Republican military man was named after a noted evangelist?

12. What Catholic candidate assured the Houston Ministerial Association that his religion would *not* be a problem?

13. What quiet New England-born president never joined a church but was "voted into" the First Congregational Church in D.C.?

14. What man, raised in the Dutch Reformed church, knew the Bible well but did not want "In God We Trust" on U.S. coins?

15. What Civil War veteran, baptized as a Presbyterian, instituted the Sunday evening "hymn sings" at the White House?

16. What member of the Disciples of Christ was the first president to meet with a pope while in office?

17. Who was reared by a Seventh-day Adventist mother, flirted with atheism, but became a Baptist?

18. What portly man admitted that as a Unitarian he did not accept the divinity of Jesus?

19. What devout Presbyterian would not conduct state business on a Sunday?

20. What president, dying from cancer, was supposedly baptized as a Methodist on his deathbed?

21. What two men formed the only team of president and vice president in which neither belonged to a church?

22. Who feared that his son's death in a train wreck was a punishment for his own lack of faith?

23. What Democrat had so many doubts about Christianity that he postponed joining a church until after leaving the White House?

24. What Virginia-born military man refused to discuss politics on Sundays?

25. Who experienced a deepening of his faith at a Tennessee camp meeting in 1833?

26. What Bible-quoting president was frequently called an "infidel" and an "open scoffer at Christianity"?

27. What Democrat, a Presbyterian pastor's son, attributed his political success to his mother's prayers?

28. What Democrat read the Bible every day and prayed every morning and night while in the White House?

29. What Quaker president chose to "affirm" instead of "swear" when he took the oath of office?

30. Who, in the 1990s, severed his lifelong ties with the Southern Baptists, claiming they had become too conservative?

31. Who surprised people by *not* appointing an ambassador to the Vatican?

32. Who met his future wife when in Sunday school when he was six years old?

33. Who postponed joining a church until he was president?

34. Which presidents rejected the pacifist teaching of the churches in which they were raised?

35. Who taught Sunday school in an Episcopal church while he was a Harvard student?

36. Who recited the Lord's Prayer after being shot by an assassin?

37. Who, while serving as ambassador to Russia, was so strict about the Sabbath that he would not dance at court balls held on Sundays?

38. Who was so strict about the Sabbath that he would not even read mail on Sundays?

39. What lifelong Presbyterian had himself baptized as a Methodist on his deathbed?

40. What well-known preacher and best-selling author officiated at Donald Trump's (first) marriage?

41. What president distanced himself from his sometimes controversial pastor, Jeremiah Wright?

Things of the Spirit (answers)

1. Harry S. Truman. The day was July 4, 1952.
2. Andrew Jackson.
3. Thomas Jefferson. He admired Jesus' teaching but could not accept the Bible's miracles. His "edited" Gospels appear in book form as *The Life and Morals of Jesus of Nazareth.*
4. Woodrow Wilson.
5. Jimmy Carter, whose sister was Ruth Carter Stapleton.
6. William McKinley.
7. Richard Nixon.
8. Franklin Roosevelt. He claimed he didn't mind being in a "goldfish bowl," but "I'll be hanged if I can say my prayers in it."
9. James A. Garfield.
10. John Quincy Adams.
11. Dwight Eisenhower. His mother named him after evangelist Dwight L. Moody.
12. John F. Kennedy.
13. Calvin Coolidge. The church and its pastor "voted him in" as a member.
14. Theodore Roosevelt.
15. Rutherford Hayes.
16. Lyndon Johnson. He met with Paul VI in 1966.
17. Warren Harding.
18. William Howard Taft.
19. Benjamin Harrison.
20. Ulysses S. Grant. Some say Grant never submitted to baptism but allowed a visiting Methodist pastor to say he had, so as to put his wife's mind at ease.
21. Abraham Lincoln and Andrew Johnson. Although both knew the Bible well, neither formally joined any church.
22. Franklin Pierce.

23. James Buchanan, who eventually joined a Presbyterian church.
24. William Henry Harrison.
25. James K. Polk.
26. Abraham Lincoln. He never joined any church, but he probably knew the Bible and quoted it more often than any other president.
27. Grover Cleveland.
28. Woodrow Wilson.
29. Herbert Hoover. Quakers are taught not to swear during an oath, but "affirming" is all right.
30. Jimmy Carter.
31. John F. Kennedy, the only Catholic president.
32. Harry S. Truman.
33. Dwight Eisenhower, who joined National Presbyterian Church in D.C.
34. Herbert Hoover and Richard Nixon (both Quakers) and Dwight Eisenhower (River Brethren).
35. Theodore Roosevelt.
36. William McKinley.
37. James Buchanan.
38. Franklin Pierce.
39. James K. Polk.
40. Norman Vincent Peale, author of *The Power of Positive Thinking* and other best-sellers.
41. Barack Obama.

Medical Matters

1. What former general carried two bullets in his body? (Hint: Tennessee)
2. Who had a grand total of one tooth at the time of his inauguration?
3. What lanky man was said to have suffered from the rare disorder known as Marfan's syndrome?

4. In what unusual locale did Grover Cleveland undergo a cancer operation?

5. What chubby New Englander suffered from constant ailments but died at age 90, one of the longest-lived presidents?

6. What man during the Civil War had his dentures accidentally thrown away by a servant?

7. What widowed Virginian permanently crippled his right wrist when he tried to leap a fence in France?

8. What dapper man suffered as president with Bright's disease, which eventually killed him?

9. What unfortunate Southern president was accused of being an alcoholic but had only one real problem, kidney stones?

10. What tiny president suffered from epilepsy?

11. Who has a facial scar due to a soccer accident in prep school?

12. What macho man was almost blind in his left eye due to a blow in a boxing match?

13. Who ran the famous Battle Creek, Michigan, sanitarium where Warren Harding sometimes went to recoup his health?

14. Who was already 240 pounds when he graduated from college?

15. What redhead suffered constantly from nasal and bronchial complaints and feared he had tuberculosis?

16. What future Democratic president was diagnosed with polio in 1921?

17. Who nearly died after a back operation and suffered constantly from back pain?

18. What ex-jock had weak knees due to old football injuries?

19. What plain-spoken man wore glasses from the age of six?

20. What New England man, who kept a detailed diary, claimed he struggled with "uncontrollable dejection of spirits"?

21. Who had such bad eyesight that he liked to read with a candle near his eyes? (Hint: Pennsylvania)

22. What bespectacled man was almost blind in his last years?

23. What ex-soldier had a heart attack while president and also had an intestinal bypass operation?

24. What Democrat was criticized for showing off his scar from gallbladder surgery?

25. Who has a bent finger as a result of an injury caused by a cotton gin?

26. What handsome president had a constant cough due to chronic bronchitis?

27. What Republican once shattered his thigh bone in a celebrity baseball game?

28. What painfully thin ex-soldier had to use a cane when he walked?

Medical Matters (answers)

1. Andrew Jackson. Both bullets were fired in duels.

2. George Washington.

3. Abraham Lincoln. The disease was unknown at the time, but later medical authors have noted Lincoln had several of its symptoms, including unusually long arms and legs, extra-long middle fingers, a sunken chest, and heart problems.

4. A yacht in New York's East River. Cleveland had a cancer in his mouth removed, and it was done aboard the yacht to avoid any publicity. The successful operation was kept a secret for over twenty years.

5. John Adams.

6. Ulysses S. Grant.

7. Thomas Jefferson. He apparently was trying to impress his lady love of the moment, artist Maria Cosway.

8. Chester Arthur. Bright's disease, a kidney ailment, was always fatal in those days.

9. Andrew Johnson. The public never got over his being drunk at his vice-presidential inauguration.

10. James Madison. It is possible that Madison's occasional seizures were not genuine epilepsy but a sort of psychosomatic disorder.

11. George H. W. Bush.

12. Theodore Roosevelt.

13. The famous (or infamous) Dr. J. P. Kellogg. (Yes, he was connected with the breakfast cereal.)

14. William Howard Taft. His weight problem throughout his life placed a strain on his heart.

15. Calvin Coolidge.

16. Franklin Roosevelt.

17. John F. Kennedy.

18. Gerald Ford, who was known to fall down in public.

19. Harry Truman.

20. John Quincy Adams. Today we would call the condition "depression."

21. James Buchanan.

22. Woodrow Wilson.

23. Dwight Eisenhower.

24. Lyndon Johnson. This got spoofed in the movie *Forrest Gump* with Gump exposing his buttock scar to Johnson.

25. Jimmy Carter.

26. Franklin Pierce.

27. Ronald Reagan.

28. Andrew Jackson.

✳   ✳   ✳

Food Fixations

In times past, in the pre-TV era when presidents weren't so much "in the fishbowl," most people knew little about what presidents liked to eat. In our tabloid era, we can't help but know some of the preferences—and oddities—of the chief executives.

1. What Republican is often remembered as "the jellybean man"?
2. What Democrat admitted he might occasionally give in to a "Big Mac attack"?
3. Who barred broccoli from the Air Force One menu?
4. What chubby president was especially fond of German food?
5. What Republican was an avid cook, noted for his steaks and vegetable soup?
6. Who was one of the first Americans to grow and eat tomatoes?
7. Who admitted to a fondness for pork rinds sprinkled with Tabasco sauce?
8. Which president was thought to have died after gorging on cherries and milk at a Fourth of July bash?
9. What military hero was so squeamish about blood that he cringed at the sight of rare meat?
10. What "sweet" plant did Theodore Roosevelt like so much he had it trucked from Long Island to D.C.?
11. What *old* president's favorite dessert was prune whip? (Hint: World War II hero)
12. Who had a Texas barbecue set up on the White House roof?
13. Who said his favorite food was pizza from the Italian Fiesta Pizzeria in Chicago?
14. What dairy item (which he smothered in ketchup) was the favorite lunch of Gerald Ford?

Food Fixations (answers)

1. Ronald Reagan. His fondness for jellybeans was rumored to increase the sales.
2. Bill Clinton.
3. George H. W. Bush, who admitted he could no longer tolerate the vegetable forced on him as a child.
4. Grover Cleveland.
5. Dwight Eisenhower.
6. Thomas Jefferson. Hardly anyone ate tomatoes in the 1700s.
7. George H. W. Bush.
8. Zachary Taylor.
9. Ulysses S. Grant, who liked his meat *very* well done.
10. Sweet potatoes.
11. Dwight Eisenhower, who, prior to Ronald Reagan, was the oldest man to serve as president.
12. Lyndon Johnson.
13. Barack Obama.
14. Cottage cheese. (Each to his own taste.)

✳   ✳   ✳

Hobbies, Pastimes, and R and R

America has had a couple of presidents who were strictly political animals, so caught up in the political game that they cultivated no outside interests. But most have had hobbies and pastimes, welcome distractions from the burdens of office. Some of these may really surprise you.

1. Who was the original American Renaissance man, dabbling in architecture, botany, engineering, and collecting a huge library?
2. What self-educated lawyer was such an avid Shakespeare fan that he could recite long passages from memory?
3. What book-loving author also loved hunting, fishing, martial arts, tennis, and nude swims in the Potomac?

4. What Democrat had a huge collection of some 25,000 stamps?

5. What cigar-addicted military man also liked to paint and draw?

6. Whose pastimes included the very British ones of fox hunting and billiards? (Hint: Virginia gentleman)

7. Who is remembered for his "poker Cabinet" with its whiskey-drinking and card-playing in the White House?

8. What bulky man was the first golfing president (and also apparently had the hobby of eating)?

9. What bespectacled president was a talented pianist and fond of classical painting?

10. What World War II navy man won enough money from poker games to finance his first run for Congress?

11. Who had a winter retreat named Glen Ora in Virginia? (Hint: handsome)

12. What intellectual played golf for exercise but admitted he disliked the game?

13. What stout president loved fishing and went hunting with a rifle named "Death and Destruction"?

14. What pudgy man took five-mile walks but mainly lived through his huge library?

15. What frontiersman loved pipe-smoking, cockfighting, and horse-breeding?

16. What quiet man enjoyed playing practical jokes on his staff?

17. What ex-military man loved landscape painting and had a studio in the White House?

18. What petite Virginia man throughout his life kept up his interest in reading Greek and Latin?

19. Who liked opera, theater, and wine, something his Whig opponents used against him during the campaign?

20. Who would take guests for 90-mph rides around his ranch?

21. What dapper president loved to have late-night suppers at the White House, followed by strolls through town?

22. What Republican admitted he liked to read newspapers but always read the comics first?

23. What book-loving president encouraged creating a White House library?

24. Who, in 1985, paid $300 to become a life member of the National Rifle Association?

25. What Southerner liked classical music enough to have it piped into the Oval Office?

26. What highly intellectual president was also remembered for his daily nude swims in the Potomac River?

27. What plantation-reared man liked to play the violin while accompanied by his wife on guitar?

28. What 20th-century president compulsively doodled while working?

29. What was Calvin Coolidge's famous reply when asked, "Mr. Coolidge, what is your hobby?"

30. Who said he liked fishing because "all men are equal before the fish"?

31. What Union veteran, who loved hunting, caused a lot of laughs when he mistakenly shot a farmer's pig?

32. What Republican as a youth played the organ at Quaker meetings and played the piano at parties?

33. What quiet man liked to play the harmonica?

34. What tall man, a good dancer, learned the "watusi" from his daughter?

35. What retired military man enjoyed nothing more than watching TV westerns with his wife and eating TV dinners?

Hobbies, Pastimes, and R and R (answers)

1. Thomas Jefferson, of course.
2. Abraham Lincoln, who also memorized the poems of Byron, Burns, and other poets.
3. Theodore Roosevelt, the proponent of "the strenuous life."
4. Franklin Roosevelt.
5. Ulysses S. Grant.
6. George Washington.
7. Warren Harding.
8. William Howard Taft.
9. Harry Truman.
10. Richard Nixon.
11. John F. Kennedy.
12. Woodrow Wilson.
13. Grover Cleveland.
14. John Adams. He did more than just read, adorning his books with all manner of marginal notes and comments.
15. Andrew Jackson.
16. Calvin Coolidge, who would do things like summon the staff with a bell, then hide under his desk.
17. Dwight Eisenhower, who said his creations were not paintings but just "daubs."
18. James Madison.
19. Martin Van Buren, called the effete "champagne" candidate, as opposed to the "hard cider" candidate, William Henry Harrison.
20. Lyndon Johnson.
21. Chester Arthur.
22. Ronald Reagan.
23. Millard Fillmore.
24. George H. W. Bush.

25. Jimmy Carter.
26. John Quincy Adams. On one occasion he had his clothes stolen while in the river.
27. John Tyler, who was quite a good violinist.
28. Ronald Reagan.
29. "Holding political office."
30. Herbert Hoover, an avid fisherman who wore a tie while fishing.
31. Benjamin Harrison.
32. Richard Nixon.
33. Calvin Coolidge.
34. Lyndon Johnson.
35. Dwight Eisenhower.

Jock Presidents

Americans like sports, and they like their presidents to be sporting—or at least to be fans. While we've had a few bookworm presidents who had zero interest in physical activity, most have cultivated some sport or another as a pastime—and under "sports" we can include "nude swims in the Potomac River."

1. What gutsy man do we associate with the phrase "the strenuous life"?
2. What Republican, a multi-sports man, played on the Yale baseball team and was an avid tennis player and jogger while president?
3. What chunky man was the first president to play golf?
4. What swim coach and lifeguard rescued a total of 77 people in the years 1926 to 1933? (Hint: two-term Republican)
5. Who was offered football contracts by both the Detroit Lions and Green Bay Packers?
6. Who swam in the White House pool daily and exercised for his chronic back problems?

7. What Republican was above-average at both golf and bowling?
8. What avid golfer, a Republican, had a putting green installed near the White House rose garden?
9. What New Englander liked horseback riding but gave up real horses for a mechanical one?
10. Who was the first president to study martial arts?
11. What Ohio man golfed twice a week but preferred poker with cigars and whiskey?
12. What Republican tossed around a medicine ball for his morning workout?
13. What Democrat was an avid swimmer and, in his college days, football player?
14. Who is the only president to appear at Wrestlemania?
15. Who, while in his 70s, enjoyed chopping wood and building fences at his Rancho de Cielo?
16. Who started the tradition of the president tossing out the first ball at the opening of baseball season?
17. What scholarly president golfed because his doctor told him to?
18. What outspoken Democrat took a two-mile morning walk, at the incredible pace of 128 steps per minute?
19. What Southerner was on the cross-country team while at the Naval Academy?
20. Who was a football star at West Point until an injury in 1912 forced him out of play?
21. What former University of Michigan football star rode an exercise bike and lifted weights in the White House?
22. What prudish president is remembered for his nude swims in the Potomac River?
23. Who liked pitching horseshoes so much that he had a horseshoe pit installed on the White House lawn?
24. Who told *Men's Health* magazine that he worked out six mornings a week, 45 minutes each time?

25. According to William Howard Taft, what game was delightful because while playing it "you cannot permit yourself to think of anything else"?

26. Who was the first president to run a marathon?

Jock Presidents (answers)

1. Theodore Roosevelt, who overcame his childhood asthma and scrawniness to become an avid boxer, hunter, and all-around jock.

2. George H. W. Bush.

3. William Howard Taft.

4. Ronald Reagan.

5. Gerald Ford.

6. John F. Kennedy.

7. Richard Nixon.

8. Dwight Eisenhower. The green was installed by the U.S. Golf Association.

9. Calvin Coolidge.

10. Appropriately enough, Theodore Roosevelt. He took up jiujitsu after a boxing match injured him severely.

11. Warren Harding.

12. Herbert Hoover.

13. Franklin Roosevelt. After being struck with polio, he gave up football but never gave up swimming.

14. Donald Trump.
15. Ronald Reagan.
16. William Howard Taft.
17. Woodrow Wilson, who disliked the game intensely.
18. Harry S. Truman.
19. Jimmy Carter.
20. Dwight Eisenhower. He was so distraught that he considered dropping out of school altogether.
21. Gerald Ford.
22. John Quincy Adams. He was still skinny-dipping at age 79. At age 58 he swam the width of the Potomac, about one mile, in one hour.
23. George H. W. Bush.
24. Barack Obama.
25. Golf.
26. George W. Bush.

✳ ✳ ✳

Things of the Spirit (Part 2)

1. Who was given a purple, velvet-bound Bible by former slaves?
2. What Southern Democrat, a Sunday school teacher, had the Secret Service code name "the Deacon"?
3. What president divides his churchgoing between Episcopal churches in Houston and Kennebunkport, Maine?
4. What early president claimed that "the studious perusal of the Sacred Book will make better citizens, better fathers, and better husbands"?
5. What preacher's son claimed he like to read "just the Bible," meaning a Bible without notes or commentaries?
6. Who carried with him a booklet, *The Necessary Duty for Family Prayer, with Prayers for Their Use*?
7. What Quaker president had read through the whole Bible by age ten?

8. What Republican said to "hold fast to the Bible as the anchor of your liberties"?

9. Who was a skeptic about the Bible but nonetheless donated money to Bible societies?

10. What military man advised his children to read from the Bible every night before going to bed?

11. Who, at his inauguration, laid his hand on the Bible used in the first inauguration of George Washington?

12. Who started the interdenominational White House prayer breakfasts? (Hint: World War II hero)

13. What Republican had a house number changed from 666 because of the satanic connections with that number?

14. What 20th-century Democrat said, "I believe in an America where religious liberty is so indivisible that an act against one church is treated as an act against all"?

15. What Republican said, "Our government makes no sense unless it is founded in a deeply felt religious faith, and I don't care what it is"?

16. What president in the 1880s raised some eyebrows by endorsing the Salvation Army?

17. Who, in 1797, told a group of ministers that "religion and morality are the essential pillars of civil society"?

18. Who, accused of being an "infidel," worshiped at Christ Episcopal Church in D.C. while president?

19. Who, though he never joined a church, rented a pew at the First Presbyterian Church in Springfield, Illinois?

20. What New Englander said, in his 80s, "I have been a church-going animal for 76 years"?

21. What frontiersman recorded in his diary that he read three to five chapters of the Bible every day?

22. What Northerner, after leaving the presidency, was kept out a church for four years because he had endorsed slavery?

23. What Union veteran was at one time a Sunday school superintendent in his Methodist church?

24. Who proclaimed a national day of humiliation "to satisfy divine displeasure"?

25. What man, later assassinated, proclaimed a day of "sorrowful submission to the will of Almighty God"?

26. What 20th-century Republican president has a minister son, a graduate of the evangelical Gordon-Conwell Seminary?

27. What Republican said "The Bible is pretty good about keeping your ego in check"?

28. What popular "positive thinking" preacher performed the wedding for Julie Nixon and David Eisenhower?

29. What recent Republican published the book *In God I Trust*?

30. What multilingual president of the 1800s read daily from the Bible in English, French, and German?

31. What future president did Theodore Roosevelt send as a representative to Pope Leo XIII in 1902?

32. What war hero joined the Presbyterian church the day after being elected president?

33. What lifelong politician from Texas often used the biblical phrase "Let us reason together"?

34. What skeptical Virginia man observed that "It does me no injury for my neighbor to say there are twenty gods or no God"?

Things of the Spirit (Part 2) (answers)

1. Abraham Lincoln, "the Great Emancipator."
2. Jimmy Carter.
3. George H. W. Bush.
4. Thomas Jefferson.
5. Grover Cleveland.
6. James Madison.
7. Herbert Hoover.
8. Ulysses S. Grant.
9. Thomas Jefferson.
10. Zachary Taylor.
11. George H. W. Bush (done in celebration of the 200th anniversary of Washington's inauguration) *and* his son George W. Bush.
12. Dwight Eisenhower.
13. Ronald Reagan. The Reagans had their house number in Bel Air, California, changed to 668. (If you're puzzled about the sinister meaning of 666, see the Bible, Book of Revelation 13:18.)
14. John F. Kennedy.
15. Dwight Eisenhower.
16. Grover Cleveland. At the time, the Salvation Army was still not accepted by many Americans.
17. George Washington.
18. Thomas Jefferson.
19. Abraham Lincoln.
20. John Adams.
21. Andrew Jackson.
22. James Buchanan. He finally was admitted to membership.
23. William McKinley.
24. John Adams. His proclamation was on May 9, 1797.
25. James Garfield.

26. Gerald Ford.

27. George W. Bush.

28. Norman Vincent Peale, author of such best-sellers as *The Power of Positive Thinking.*

29. Ronald Reagan. The book is a collection of his public statements on religion and morality.

30. John Quincy Adams, who made it a point to read through the entire Bible once a year.

31. William Howard Taft, who asked the pope for the Roman Catholic church to give up its thousands of acres of farm land in the Philippines.

32. Dwight Eisenhower.

33. Lyndon Johnson.

34. Thomas Jefferson, who added, "It neither picks my pocket nor breaks my leg."

✸ 7 ✸

Cabinet, Congress, Court

Presidential Furniture: The Cabinet

No man is an island, and no president has to go it alone, politically speaking. From George Washington on, the presidents have had their official circle of advisors—some of them astute men of wisdom, some of them political hacks, and some of them just old buddies that were being done a favor. Considering that some cabinet members served longer than many presidents, their effect on American life has been amazing. (No one would doubt, for example, that cabinet men like Henry Clay and Daniel Webster had more influence on history than a president like, say, Franklin Pierce.)

1. What lanky, witty man would read his cabinet humorous essays from authors like Petroleum V. Nasby?

2. What Clinton cabinet member was charged with mishandling the Branch Davidian affair?

3. What cabinet member's firing led to the impeachment of Andrew Johnson?

4. In 1790 what cabinet officer wrote his *Report on the Public Credit*?

5. What Secretary of State was largely responsible for the purchase of Alaska from Russia?

6. What future president resigned from the cabinet in 1793 over differences with Treasury Secretary Alexander Hamilton? (Hint: Virginia)

7. Who was notorious for his unofficial "Kitchen Cabinet" of advisors? (Hint: Tennessee)

8. What wife of a recent Republican candidate served as Secretary of Transportation?

9. What Southern notable served as Secretary of War under his friend Franklin Pierce?

10. The first televised cabinet meeting was under which president?

11. What three-time Democratic presidential candidate was Woodrow Wilson's Secretary of State?

12. To protect "our most important national investment," Jimmy Carter signed a bill in 1979 creating which cabinet department?

13. Who were the two ever-feuding members of George Washington's cabinet?

14. Who was first to appoint a black woman as Secretary of State?

15. What Virginia-born president was on board the ship *Princeton* when an explosion injured some of his cabinet members?

16. What future president, while serving as Secretary of State, granted an ambassador's request for concubines?

17. Brassy, controversial Martha Mitchell was the wife of which Nixon cabinet member?

18. What Democrat's first cabinet included three Republicans—and a woman?

19. Under what president did cabinet members' wives ostracize the infamous Peggy Eaton?

20. What Ohio-born president once gave artificial respiration to his Secretary of the Navy?

21. What Republican opened his cabinet meetings with a moment of silent prayer?

22. With what major scandal do we associate Albert Fall, Warren Harding's Secretary of the Interior?

23. What wealthy man was Treasury Secretary under Coolidge and Hoover, and later hounded by Franklin Roosevelt?

24. What renowned World War II general did Harry Truman make Secretary of State?

25. What president did anti-Communist Secretary of State John Foster Dulles serve under?

26. What foreign policy whiz did Gerald Ford inherit from Richard Nixon?

27. What cabinet member was attacked and almost killed as part of the plot to assassinate Lincoln?

28. What cabinet member of Washington did John Adams refer to as "that Creole bastard"?

29. In 1843 Daniel Webster resigned as what president's Secretary of State?

30. Who had twice-weekly poker games with the group he called his "Poker Cabinet"?

31. What World War II general did Congress exempt from the rule about military men *not* serving as Secretary of Defense?

32. Who had his own brother as his Attorney General?

33. What member of George W. Bush's cabinet continued in the same post under Obama?

34. What Reagan cabinet member tried to negotiate a settlement between Britain and Argentina in the Falkland Islands crisis?

210 ✸ THE COMPLETE BOOK OF PRESIDENTIAL TRIVIA

Presidential Furniture: The Cabinet (answers)

1. Abraham Lincoln.
2. The often-controversial Attorney General Janet Reno.
3. Edwin Stanton, Secretary of War.
4. Alexander Hamilton, George Washington's Secretary of the Treasury.
5. William Seward, who served under Lincoln and Johnson.
6. Thomas Jefferson, Secretary of State.
7. Andrew Jackson. *All* presidents have, of course, had advisors who were not cabinet members.
8. Elizabeth Dole, who served under George H. W. Bush.
9. Jefferson Davis, later to be president of the Confederacy.
10. Dwight Eisenhower, on October 25, 1954.
11. William Jennings Bryan.
12. Education. Prior to this, education was part of the Health, Education, and Welfare Department. The creation of the Education Department was Carter's payoff to the powerful teachers' unions that supported him.
13. Thomas Jefferson, Secretary of State, and Alexander Hamilton, Secretary of the Treasury. Both eventually resigned.
14. George W. Bush, who appointed Condoleezza Rice.
15. John Tyler.
16. John Quincy Adams. This is remarkable, considering how prudish Adams was, but he did indeed procure concubines for the ambassador from Tunisia.
17. Attorney General John Mitchell.
18. Franklin Roosevelt's.
19. Andrew Jackson. Her husband was Jackson's Secretary of War and because Peggy was regarded as a loose woman, the other cabinet wives would have nothing to do with her, which infuriated Jackson.
20. Benjamin Harrison. His Navy Secretary, Benjamin Tracy, almost suffocated in a house fire and Harrison revived him.

21. Dwight Eisenhower.
22. Teapot Dome.
23. Andrew Mellon, whom FDR despised.
24. George Marshall.
25. Dwight Eisenhower.
26. Secretary of State Henry Kissinger.
27. William Seward, Secretary of State, who was stabbed by one of John Wilkes Booth's accomplices.
28. Alexander Hamilton, Secretary of the Treasury. Since Hamilton was illegitimate, Adams was using "bastard" in the literal sense.
29. John Tyler's. Webster was the last of Tyler's cabinet to resign.
30. Warren Harding.
31. George C. Marshall, who served briefly in that post under Harry Truman.
32. John F. Kennedy, who had to endure some criticism for making his younger brother Bobby his Attorney General.
33. Robert Gates, Secretary of Defense.
34. Secretary of State Alexander Haig.

The Men and Women in My Cabinet

Would you recognize the president by seeing the names of some of his cabinet members? Give it a shot. The lists below contain some very famous—and some very obscure—figures from America's past.

1. Richard Cheney, Elizabeth Dole, Nicholas Brady
2. Thomas Jefferson, Alexander Hamilton, Edmund Randolph
3. James Monroe, Caesar Rodney, William Eustis
4. John Ashcroft, Elaine Chao, Donald Rumsfeld
5. James Buchanan, George Bancroft, Cave Johnson
6. Jefferson Davis, Caleb Cushing, William L. Marcy

7. Henry Kissinger, Melvin Laird, John Mitchell
8. John Foster Dulles, William P. Rogers, Oveta Culp Hobby
9. Eric Holder, Ray LaHood, Hillary Clinton
10. William Bennett, Alexander Haig, James G. Watt
11. Cordell Hull, Henry A. Wallace, Henry L. Stimson
12. Charles Evans Hughes, Will Hays, Albert Fall
13. James Blaine, William Windom, John Wanamaker
14. John Hay, Elihu Root, James R. Garfield
15. Robert Kennedy, Dean Rusk, Orville Freeman
16. Henry L. Stimson, Andrew Mellon, Charles Francis Adams
17. William Jennings Bryan, Carter Glass, William Redfield
18. John Sherman, Lyman Gage, Elihu Root
19. William Seward, Edwin Stanton, Henry Stanbery
20. Robert Reich, Janet Reno, Bill Richardson
21. Frank Kellogg, Herbert Hoover, Andrew Mellon
22. Reverdy Johnson, Thomas Ewing, Jacob Collamer
23. Thomas Bayard, Lucius Q. C. Lamar, Augustus Garland
24. Dean Rusk, Ramsey Clark, Clark Clifford
25. Elihu Washburne, William T. Sherman, Zachariah Chandler
26. Edwin Stanton, William Seward, Salmon P. Chase
27. Cyrus Vance, Griffin Bell, Cecil Andrus
28. Daniel Webster, John C. Calhoun, John Y. Mason
29. Henry Clay, Richard Rush, Peter Porter
30. Robert Lincoln, Walter Gresham, Benjamin Brewster
31. Philander Knox, Henry L. Stimson, Frank Hitchcock
32. Henry Kissinger, Earl Butz, Caspar Weinberger
33. Dean Acheson, James Forestal, Harold Ickes
34. John Sherman, Carl Schurz, Nathan Goff

35. Benjamin F. Butler, Joel Poinsett, Levi Woodbury
36. John Quincy Adams, John C. Calhoun, Richard Rush
37. James Madison, Henry Dearborn, Caesar Rodney
38. Martin Van Buren, John Eaton, Roger Taney
39. John Marshall, Oliver Wolcott, Charles Lee

The Men and Women in My Cabinet (answers)

1. George H. W. Bush.
2. George Washington.
3. James Madison.
4. George W. Bush.
5. James K. Polk.
6. Franklin Pierce.
7. Richard Nixon.
8. Dwight Eisenhower.
9. Barack Obama.
10. Ronald Reagan.
11. Franklin Roosevelt.
12. Warren Harding.
13. Benjamin Harrison.
14. Theodore Roosevelt.

15. John F. Kennedy.
16. Herbert Hoover.
17. Woodrow Wilson.
18. William McKinley.
19. Andrew Johnson.
20. Bill Clinton.
21. Calvin Coolidge.
22. Zachary Taylor.
23. Grover Cleveland.
24. Lyndon Johnson.
25. Ulysses S. Grant.
26. Abraham Lincoln.
27. Jimmy Carter.
28. John Tyler.
29. John Quincy Adams.
30. Chester Arthur.
31. William Howard Taft.
32. Gerald Ford.
33. Harry Truman.
34. Rutherford Hayes.
35. Martin Van Buren.
36. James Monroe.
37. Thomas Jefferson.
38. Andrew Jackson.
39. John Adams.

Adding Furniture: New Cabinet Positions

Like everything else in the federal government, the cabinet has grown—*a lot*—from the original small group that advised George

Washington. Departments have been added, split up, and had their names changed, growing from the time the cabinet could have met in a phone booth (had there been any phone booths, that is).

1. How many posts were there in George Washington's original cabinet?

2. What new position was added under John Adams, first filled by Benjamin Stoddert? (Hint: water)

3. The position of Postmaster General was added under what two-term president? (Hint: check your wallet)

4. Under Zachary Taylor, Thomas Ewing filled what new position? (Hint: woodsy)

5. The post of Secretary of Agriculture was added under what two-term Democrat?

6. What new double-billed post was added under Theodore Roosevelt, in 1903?

7. What department was split into two during Wilson's presidency?

8. What two departments merged to become one under Harry Truman?

9. What "helpful" department was added in 1953, under Dwight Eisenhower?

10. Two new departments, the Department of Transportation and the Department of Housing and Urban Development were added under what Democrat?

11. Under Richard Nixon and a man named Red Blount, which department got "de-Cabinetized"?

12. In 1979, under Carter, the Department of Health, Education, and Welfare became what?

13. Who created the Department of Homeland Security?

14. The Department of Veterans Affairs was added under what World War II veteran?

15. Who asked for a new cabinet post of Secretary of Commerce and Industries, but instead got a Secretary of Commerce and Labor?

Adding Furniture: New Cabinet Positions (answers)

1. Four—Secretary of State, Secretary of the Treasury, Secretary of War, and Attorney General.

2. Secretary of the Navy. Stoddert served 1798-1801.

3. Andrew Jackson. There had been Postmasters General earlier, but not as part of the cabinet. The first in the cabinet, under Jackson, was William T. Barry, who assumed his office in 1829.

4. Secretary of the Interior.

5. Grover Cleveland. Norman Colman served barely a month at the end of Cleveland's first term, replaced by (thanks to Benjamin Harrison) a Republican.

6. Secretary of Commerce and Labor. The first was George Cortelyou.

7. Commerce and Labor became two instead of one, as of 1913.

8. War and Navy became Defense, with former Navy Secretary James Forrestal as first Defense Secretary.

9. Health, Education, and Welfare, with Oveta Culp Hobby as first Secretary.

10. Lyndon Johnson. In the past, Transportation had fallen under the Commerce umbrella.

11. The mail. Winton "Red" Blount was the last Postmaster General to serve in a cabinet. He oversaw the department as it converted to the U.S. Postal Service.

12. Health and Human Services, plus the new Department of Education.

13. George W. Bush.

14. George H. W. Bush, in 1989. The first Secretary was Edward Derwinski.

15. Theodore Roosevelt.

Presidential Furniture: The Cabinet (Part 2)

1. What 20th-century Republican president's portrait did Ronald Reagan hang in the Cabinet room?

2. What did Andrew Johnson send Treasury Secretary Hugh McCulloch to investigate at Fort Monroe in Virginia?

3. James Watt, a sometimes controversial Secretary of the Interior, served under what Republican?

4. Who appointed the first female Secretary of State?

5. The 1823 Monroe Doctrine was not the work of President Monroe but of his Secretary of State, who was later a president. Who?

6. The opinionated Navy Secretary Gideon Welles, famous for his Washington diary, served under what Republican of the 1800s?

7. What noted House leader from Kentucky did John Quincy Adams make his Secretary of State?

8. Who fumbled for his glasses at a cabinet meeting and said, "I have already grown gray in the service of my country, now I am growing blind"?

9. What cabinet member under Lyndon Johnson has been often criticized for his mishandling of the Vietnam War?

10. What woman, appointed by Franklin Roosevelt, holds the record as the longest-serving cabinet member ever?

11. Lauro Cavazos, the first Hispanic to serve in a cabinet, was appointed by which Republican?

12. What Reagan cabinet member later became a best-selling author with *The Book of Virtues* and other books?

13. What exercise fanatic tired his cabinet by taking them on long hikes?

14. What 20th-century Republican wanted cabinet members to hold seats in Congress?

15. What Postmaster General under Warren Harding later became the "moral watchdog" of the movie industry?

16. Calvin Coolidge's Secretary of State, Frank Kellogg, won what international prize?

17. Whose cabinet saw several of its members depart to serve the Confederacy?

18. What Union war hero served briefly as Grant's Secretary of War?

19. What son of a famous president served as Chester Arthur's Secretary of War?

20. Millionaire John Wanamaker, Postmaster General under Benjamin Harrison, is associated with what major city?

21. John Hay, Secretary of State in McKinley's cabinet, had been private secretary to what wartime president?

22. Bainbridge Colby, Secretary of State for Woodrow Wilson, refused to recognize the revolutionary government in what huge country?

23. What international sports trophy is connected with Calvin Coolidge's Secretary of War?

24. What famous (and perhaps infamous) federal agency head was first appointed by Harlan Stone, one of Coolidge's cabinet members? (Hint: investigate)

25. Andrew Mellon, Secretary of the Treasury under three presidents, is remembered for donating what to Washington, D.C.?

26. What FDR appointee served the longest term as Secretary of State?

27. What World War II general devised the European Recovery Plan while serving as Secretary of State?

28. According to Defense Secretary Charles E. Wilson, "What was good for our country was good for General Motors, and vice versa." Under which president did Wilson serve?

29. What former member of the George W. Bush cabinet endorsed the Democratic candidate in 2008?

30. What Attorney General of Richard Nixon's served 19 months in prison for his connections with the Watergate break-in?

31. Agriculture Secretary Earl Butz, fired for telling a racist joke, served which two Republicans?

32. Caspar Weinberger, Defense Secretary under Reagan, pressed for the Strategic Defense Initiative, better known as what? (Hint: a popular movie)

33. What brother of a famous Civil War general served as Hayes's Treasury Secretary and McKinley's Secretary of State?

34. Who appointed John Ashcroft, who had lost his Senate race to a dead man, as Attorney General?

Presidential Furniture: The Cabinet (Part 2) (answers)

1. Calvin Coolidge's. Reagan was a big fan of Coolidge's "limited government" philosophy.

2. The treatment of its most famous prisoner, former Confederate president Jefferson Davis. Johnson wanted to ensure that Davis wasn't treated too harshly.

3. Ronald Reagan.

4. Bill Clinton, who appointed Madeleine Albright.

5. John Quincy Adams.

6. Abraham Lincoln.

7. Henry Clay.

8. George Washington.

9. Defense Secretary Robert McNamara.

10. Frances Perkins, appointed Secretary of Labor in 1933, holding that office until 1945.

11. Ronald Reagan, who made him Secretary of Education in 1988. Cavazos was a Democrat.

12. William Bennett, Secretary of Education.

13. Theodore Roosevelt, apostle of "the strenuous life."

14. William Howard Taft. Note that he wanted them as *non-voting* members of Congress, present there so they could give input relating to their particular departments. He did not get his wish anyway.

15. Will Hays, whose name will forever be attached to Hollywood's Production Code (better known as "the Hays Code"), the movie industry's self-imposed code regarding movies' portrayals of violence, morals, and religion.

16. The Nobel Peace Prize. Kellogg won it in 1929 for having negotiated the Kellogg-Briand Pact.

17. James Buchanan's. They were reacting not to anything Buchanan had done, but to their home states seceding from the Union and forming the Confederacy.

18. William Tecumseh Sherman.

19. Robert Lincoln, son of Abraham.

20. Philadelphia, home to the chain of Wanamaker department stores.

21. Abraham Lincoln.

22. Russia (or, as it was called after the Revolution, the Soviet Union). Like most nations, the U.S. was slow to accept the Communist regime that took over Russia. In fact, the U.S. did not officially recognize the Soviet Union until 1933.

23. The Davis Cup. Coolidge's Secretary of War 1925-29 was Dwight F. Davis, a tennis player who in 1900 had donated the Davis Cup as an international trophy.

24. J. Edgar Hoover, who at age 29 was appointed by Attorney General Stone to head the Federal Bureau of Investigation, a post he held for decades.

25. His huge art collection, which was the foundation for the National Gallery of Art in Washington.

26. Cordell Hull, who served from 1933 to 1944.

27. George C. Marshall, which is why the plan is still known as the Marshall Plan.

28. Dwight Eisenhower. Wilson had been president of General Motors prior to serving in the cabinet. His words passed into the language as "What's good for General Motors is good for the country."

29. Colin Powell, who had served as Secretary of State.

30. John Mitchell.

31. Richard Nixon and Gerald Ford.

32. Star Wars.

33. John Sherman, brother of General William Tecumseh Sherman.

34. George W. Bush. Ashcroft lost his 2000 Senate race to Mel Carnahan who had died in a plane crash a few weeks earlier. The Senate seat went to Carnahan's widow.

✷   ✷   ✷

The Quarrelsome (and Sometimes Cooperative) Congress

"Gridlock" only recently found its way into our political jargon, but it existed long before. Our Founding Fathers would probably say, "Precisely what we had in mind." The founders' concept of "balance of power" allowed for gridlock, and even encouraged it, making sure that the Congress could apply the brakes to what the president wanted—and vice versa, of course. Frustrating and amusing as it has sometimes been, it's a system we should be proud of.

1. What impeached man was acquitted by a Senate vote of 35 to 18?

2. What House Speaker pushed for the Contract with America during the Clinton years?

3. In 1867 Congress declared Nebraska the 37th state, overriding what president's veto?

4. Congress overrode only nine of what Democratic president's record 935 vetoes?

5. Andrew Jackson won the popular *and* electoral vote in the 1824 election, so why did John Quincy Adams become president?

6. What frugal Republican vetoed a bill that gave a bonus to World War I veterans?

7. What Democrat called the Eightieth Congress the "Do-Nothing Congress" and "the worst Congress in history"?

8. Who refused to sign Congress's vengeful, anti-Southern Reconstruction Bill?

9. William McKinley demanded Congress's "forceful intervention" on what island?

10. Who tried to "pack" the Supreme Court with new justices because the old Court kept declaring Congress's acts unconstitutional?

11. What World War II hero saw the Republicans win both houses of Congress when he was elected?

12. In July 1866 Congress created the new rank of "general of the armies" for what future president?

13. Who submitted to Congress a $17 billion European Recovery Program?

14. Republican Congressman Joe Wilson of South Carolina shouted, "You lie!" during which president's speech?

15. What tall president is shown, in a famous photo, kissing short Speaker of the House Sam Rayburn on top of his bald head?

16. What military hero, at the end of his second term, told Congress that "failures have been errors of judgment, not of intent"?

17. What disputed election was decided by a fifteen-member congressional commission?

18. Who turned his Ph.D. thesis into the book *Congressional Government*?
19. Who had his "Fair Deal" program almost totally rejected by Congress?
20. What nation's predatory U-boats provoked Woodrow Wilson to ask Congress to declare war on Germany?
21. Who first ordered the reading aloud in Congress of George Washington's Farewell Address?
22. What famous purchase, Jefferson's pride and joy, did Congress approve in October 1803?
23. What was the core of the Truman Doctrine, announced to Congress in 1947?
24. Who persuaded Congress to pass the Embargo Act, forbidding U.S. ships to leave for foreign ports?
25. In June 1950, Truman committed U.S. troops to what Asian nation?
26. What future president produced drafts of the Bill of Rights for Congress in 1789?
27. Whose immense library, sold to the government in 1815, was the foundation for the Library of Congress?
28. Who supported Congress's plan to set up a colony of freed blacks in Africa, to be called Liberia?
29. Who was the first man forced to have congressional approval to serve as vice president?
30. Who, in 1849, pushed Congress to admit California as a state immediately?
31. What famous Speaker of the House was a longtime enemy of Andrew Jackson?
32. What president's son became "Mr. Republican" in the Senate?
33. What president's proposed League of Nations was strongly opposed by Senate powerhouse Henry Cabot Lodge?

34. What famous committee was chaired by Senator Sam Ervin?

35. Who informed Congress that whenever the safety or interest of white Americans was at stake, Congress could "occupy and possess any part of Indian territory"?

36. What famous doctrine was announced to Congress in December 1823?

37. Who declared that even though "Congress will push me to raise taxes," he never would?

38. What 20th-century Republican announced to the Senate that he was "moderate in domestic affairs, conservative in fiscal affairs"?

39. What act led James K. Polk to tell Congress that "the cup of forbearance has been exhausted"?

40. Who, after delivering a State of the Union address, kissed Democratic Senator Joe Lieberman of Connecticut?

41. What Southern presidential widow, formerly a Confederate citizen, was granted a lifetime pension from Congress in 1882?

42. Who appeared before a Senate subcommittee to give assurance that his wife was not a Confederate spy?

The Quarrelsome (and Sometimes Cooperative) Congress (answers)

1. Andrew Johnson, the *first* president to be impeached by Congress.
2. Newt Gingrich.
3. Andrew Johnson's.
4. Franklin Roosevelt's.
5. Because no candidate won a clear majority, the House decided the vote, and the House chose Adams.
6. Calvin Coolidge. In this case, Congress overrode the veto.
7. Harry Truman.
8. Abraham Lincoln.
9. Cuba.
10. Franklin Roosevelt, who had Congress on his side, but not (for several years) the Supreme Court under Chief Justice Charles Evans Hughes.
11. Dwight Eisenhower.
12. Ulysses S. Grant.
13. Harry Truman.
14. Barack Obama's speech.
15. Lyndon Johnson.
16. Ulysses S. Grant.
17. The 1876 election, in which, most likely, Democrat Samuel Tilden beat Republican Rutherford Hayes. Because of the disputed election returns, Congress—dominated by Republicans—gave the election to Hayes.
18. Woodrow Wilson. Somehow he managed to write the book without ever having set foot in the Capitol.
19. Harry Truman.
20. Germany's.
21. His successor, John Adams. It was done in February in commemoration of Washington's birthday.

22. The Louisiana Purchase.
23. To support free peoples who were resisting "armed minorities or outside pressure."
24. Thomas Jefferson. The Embargo Act proved to be a disaster.
25. Korea. Truman did so without getting prior authorization from Congress.
26. James Madison.
27. Thomas Jefferson.
28. James Monroe, which is why the capital of Liberia is named Monrovia.
29. Gerald Ford, appointed by Nixon to replace Spiro Agnew. Both Senate and House approved Ford.
30. Zachary Taylor.
31. Henry Clay.
32. William Howard Taft, father of Robert Taft.
33. Woodrow Wilson.
34. The Watergate Committee, sometimes called the Ervin Committee, looking into the transgressions of Richard Nixon.
35. Andrew Jackson.
36. The Monroe Doctrine, telling European nations not to meddle in American affairs. It was named for President Monroe, though it was the work of diplomat (and future president) John Quincy Adams.
37. George H. W. Bush, who followed up with his famous words, "No new taxes."
38. Gerald Ford.
39. Some Mexicans killed some Americans near the Rio Grande which led (as Polk hoped) to war with Mexico.
40. George W. Bush, in 2005.
41. Julia, widow of John Tyler. Since Tyler was a Confederate when he died in 1862, the federal government was slow to show kindness to his family.
42. Abraham Lincoln. Mary Lincoln had brothers in the Confederate army and was presumed by many to be a Southern sympathizer.

✻   ✻   ✻

The Prez and the Court

Did our founders foresee the day when the Supreme Court would wield as much power as it now does? Hard to say. They did foresee that the Court and the presidents would be forever in a kind of love-hate relationship—that wonderful "balance of power" thing that makes the American system so good. The story of the presidents, the people they appointed to the Supreme Court, and the sometimes thorny relations involved is quite interesting.

1. What former Republican president was appointed to the Supreme Court in 1921? (Hint: chubby)

2. What early president "packed" the Supreme Court with Federalists just before leaving office?

3. What was the distinction of Louis Brandeis, appointed to the Court by Woodrow Wilson in 1916?

4. What Democratic president pushed the Judiciary Reorganization Bill, designed to pack the Court with men sympathetic to his policies?

5. Who resigned from the Court to run as a Republican against Woodrow Wilson in 1916?

6. What post was William Howard Taft holding when first invited to become a Supreme Court justice?

7. What tight-lipped man had Chief Justice Harlan Stone as his closest advisor?

8. Who was pleased that seven of the nine Supreme Court justices were his appointees?

9. What Democrat wanted Justice William O. Douglas as his running mate?

10. What president proposed in the 1800s that Supreme Court justices be elected to twelve-year terms?

11. In July 1974, what did the Supreme Court order Richard Nixon to turn over to a prosecutor?

12. What controversial Supreme Court decision was handed down during James Buchanan's term?

13. What was notable about Ronald Reagan's first appointee to the Supreme Court?

14. Whose sexual harassment suit against Bill Clinton was allowed to proceed by the Supreme Court?

15. What man is still remembered as Reagan's Supreme Court appointee that the Senate rejected as too conservative?

16. What long-term chief justice was appointed to the Court by Andrew Jackson and survived long enough to swear in Abraham Lincoln?

17. Who was president when the Supreme Court ordered the breakup of Standard Oil?

18. Who, appointed by John Adams, served the longest term as chief justice?

19. Who was the only president to appoint more than one chief justice?

20. Who appointed his Secretary of the Treasury, Salmon Chase, to be chief justice?

21. The first conservative black member of the Court was appointed by what Republican?

22. Who was president when the Court made its infamous *Roe v. Wade* decision?

23. Under what president of the 1800s was the membership of the court fixed at nine?

24. Under George Washington, how many justices did the original Supreme Court have?

25. In 1969, Abe Fortas, appointed by Lyndon Johnson, became the first justice to do what?

26. What chief justice, appointed by Washington, resigned to serve as governor of New York?

27. In 1803 Justice Samuel Chase was impeached by the House for his vicious attacks on which president?

28. Bushrod Washington, a nephew of George, was appointed to the Court by which later president?

29. What future president declined James Madison's offer of a place on the Supreme Court?

30. Which four presidents appointed no justices to the Court?

31. What future Democratic president declined James K. Polk's offer of a place on the Court?

32. Justice John Campbell, who resigned from the Court in 1861 to serve the Confederacy, had been appointed by which president from New England?

33. What former cabinet member of Lincoln presided over Andrew Johnson's impeachment trial?

34. Lucius L. Q. Lamar, a former Confederate, barely got confirmed by the Senate. Which president appointed him?

35. What son of a famous Massachusetts author was appointed to the Court by Theodore Roosevelt?

36. Hugo Black of Alabama, controversial because of having been in the KKK, was appointed by which Democrat?

37. Robert Jackson, appointed to the Court by FDR, was famous in what post-World War II trials?

38. What former pro football player did John F. Kennedy appoint?

39. Thurgood Marshall, the first black ever to serve on the Court, was appointed by which Democrat?

40. What conservative appointee of Richard Nixon was made chief justice by Ronald Reagan?

41. What president was vexed because Chief Justice John Marshall acquitted Aaron Burr of treason?

42. Harriet Miers was the friend and controversial appointee of which president?

43. What was the distinction of appointee Sonia Sotomayor?

The Prez and the Court (answers)

1. William Howard Taft, who (everyone agrees) was better on the Court than in the White House.

2. John Adams, who was not only supporting his party, but trying hard to vex his successor, Thomas Jefferson.

3. He was the first Jew appointed to the Court.

4. Franklin Roosevelt, who was vexed because the Court under Charles Evan Hughes was ruling many of his policies unconstitutional. He wanted 15 justices on the Court (which meant several new men, all appointed by him), but Congress nixed this.

5. Charles Evan Hughes, who was egged on by his old friend Theodore Roosevelt. Hughes lost to Wilson but was reappointed to the Court in 1930 and was chief justice.

6. Governor of the Philippines, a post that Taft rather liked. This was in 1901; twenty years later, Taft accepted his appointment to be chief justice.

7. Calvin Coolidge.

8. Franklin Roosevelt. This became true in 1941.

9. Harry Truman. Douglas claimed he didn't "want to be a number two man to a number two man."

10. Andrew Johnson. The Congress, which opposed Johnson at every turn, nixed this.

11. The infamous Watergate-related tapes.

12. The Dred Scott decision, which heated up the slavery issue.

13. She was the first woman on the court, Sandra Day O'Connor.

14. Paula Jones'.

15. Robert Bork. The word "borked" has entered the political lexicon, referring to Senate liberals rejecting an appointee they see as too conservative.

16. Roger Taney of Maryland. Taney served 1836-64.

17. William Howard Taft.

18. John Marshall.

19. George Washington, who appointed three: John Jay, John Rutledge, and Oliver Ellsworth.

20. Abraham Lincoln, who found Chase less troublesome on the Court than in Lincoln's cabinet.

21. George H. W. Bush. The appointee was Clarence Thomas.

22. Richard Nixon. It was 1973.

23. Ulysses S. Grant. The year was 1869.

24. Six—a chief justice and five associate justices.

25. Resign. Appointed by Johnson in 1965, Fortas was caught up in a financial scandal.

26. The first chief justice, John Jay.

27. Thomas Jefferson. The Senate, however, failed to impeach Chase, who is the only Supreme Court justice (so far) to have been impeached.

28. John Adams.

29. John Quincy Adams.

30. William Henry Harrison, Zachary Taylor, Andrew Johnson (he tried to appoint, but was blocked by a stubborn Congress), and Jimmy Carter. With the exception of Carter, all these were "short-termers," presidents who served less than a full four-year term.

31. James Buchanan.

32. Franklin Pierce. For his service in Jefferson Davis's administration, Campbell was sentenced to four months in prison after the South's defeat.

33. Salmon P. Chase, who (historians agree) was very fair to the besieged president.

34. Grover Cleveland, in 1888. Lamar had been in Cleveland's cabinet.

35. Oliver Wendell Holmes, Jr. Appropriately, Holmes, appointed by a very colorful (and controversial) president, proved to be one of the most colorful (and controversial) members of the Supreme Court.

36. Franklin Roosevelt.

37. The Nuremberg trials of Nazi war criminals.

38. Byron "Whizzer" White, who had served as deputy attorney general under Robert Kennedy.

39. Lyndon Johnson.

40. William Rehnquist.

41. Thomas Jefferson. He and Marshall were of different parties, and he was probably correct in thinking that the acquittal of Burr (who *was* treasonous) was a direct slap at Jefferson himself.

42. George W. Bush. She eventually withdrew.

43. She was the first Hispanic woman on the court.

CHAPTER

✳ 8 ✳

The Political Life

Who Were My Vice Presidents?

Plural, you say? Indeed. Although recently two-term presidents kept the same vice president for both terms, this wasn't always so in the past. For the vice presidents below, name the president they served under.

1. Spiro Agnew, Gerald Ford
2. John Nance Garner, Henry A. Wallace, Harry Truman
3. Dan Quayle
4. Nelson Rockefeller
5. Lyndon Johnson
6. Alben Barkley
7. Richard Cheney
8. Thomas Hendricks, Adlai E. Stevenson
9. John C. Calhoun, Martin Van Buren
10. Hannibal Hamlin, Andrew Johnson
11. John C. Calhoun
12. John Adams
13. Charles G. Dawes
14. George M. Dallas
15. Thomas Jefferson

16. William R. D. King
17. Schuyler Colfax, Henry Wilson
18. Charles W. Fairbanks
19. Hubert Humphrey
20. Aaron Burr, George Clinton
21. John Tyler
22. George Clinton, Eldridge Gerry
23. Chester Arthur
24. Thomas R. Marshall
25. Garrett Hobart, Theodore Roosevelt
26. Richard Nixon
27. Al Gore
28. Levi P. Morton
29. John Breckinridge
30. Daniel Tompkins
31. Richard M. Johnson
32. Millard Fillmore
33. William A. Wheeler
34. Joe Biden
35. Walter Mondale
36. George H. W. Bush
37. Calvin Coolidge
38. James S. Sherman
39. Charles Curtis.

Who Were My Vice Presidents? (answers)

1. Richard Nixon.
2. Franklin Roosevelt.
3. George H. W. Bush.
4. Gerald Ford.
5. John F. Kennedy.
6. Harry Truman.
7. George W. Bush.
8. Grover Cleveland.
9. Andrew Jackson.
10. Abraham Lincoln.
11. John Quincy Adams.
12. George Washington.
13. Calvin Coolidge.
14. James K. Polk.
15. John Adams.
16. Franklin Pierce.
17. Ulysses S. Grant.
18. Theodore Roosevelt.
19. Lyndon Johnson.
20. Thomas Jefferson.
21. William Henry Harrison.
22. James Madison.
23. James Garfield.
24. Woodrow Wilson.
25. William McKinley.
26. Dwight Eisenhower.
27. Bill Clinton.
28. Benjamin Harrison.

29. James Buchanan.
30. James Monroe.
31. Martin Van Buren.
32. Zachary Taylor.
33. Rutherford Hayes.
34. Barack Obama.
35. Jimmy Carter.
36. Ronald Reagan.
37. Warren Harding.
38. William Howard Taft.
39. Herbert Hoover.

✳   ✳   ✳

Meeting the Press

Ah, freedom of the press—one of the glories of our political life, something politicians claim to love . . . that is, until the press proves to be a thorn in their sides, which happens quite often. While some presidents have managed to make the media love them, no one has been totally immune from media attacks.

1. What scandal-plagued Republican was quoted as saying "The press is the enemy"?
2. What Democrat sparked some controversy during campaign season when he told *Playboy* he had committed adultery "in his heart" many times?
3. How did reporter Anne Royall get an interview with the skinny-dipping John Quincy Adams?
4. What popular magazine featured Richard Nixon on its cover a record fifty-five times?
5. What name did journalists give to the torrent of new legislation passed after Franklin Roosevelt took office?
6. Who had shoes hurled at him and was called a "dog" by an Iraqi journalist?

7. What member of the Nixon administration called journalists "nattering nabobs of negativism"?

8. What Republican held the first televised presidential press conference?

9. What president, according to the *National Journal*, was the son of "a common prostitute, brought to this country by British soldiers"?

10. What sort of novels did the press criticize Eisenhower for reading?

11. The infamous "Zimmerman Telegram," published in newspapers, helped spark the U.S. entry into what war?

12. Who admitted his wealthy father had purchased the support of the *Boston Post*?

13. What Democrat played poker with journalists and urged them to give men in his administration "a hard time"?

14. Who, on April 12, 1945, told journalists, "Pray for me, boys"?

15. What back-slapping president began the habit of calling reporters by their first names?

16. What glaring error was a headline of the *Chicago Tribune* in November 1948?

17. What wartime president was the first to hold regular press conferences?

18. What president did the press accuse of promoting "Piety on the Potomac"?

19. What Democrat lamented that "I have to read the newspapers to find out about American foreign policy"?

20. What Republican had read through three major newspapers by 7:30 each morning?

21. What Republican admitted he liked to read the comics section of a newspaper first?

22. What was on the slips of paper Calvin Coolidge handed to 30 journalists on August 2, 1927?

23. Who, in the 1950s, published articles in *Life, Look,* and other magazines?

24. What president endured continual press abuse from Tennessee newspaper publisher "Parson" Brownlow?

25. Who, in the 1790s, wrote newspaper articles under the pen name "Helvidius"?

26. Who met her future husband at a Washington party when she was a young journalist?

27. What presidential couple received a lashing by the press for their "adulterous union"?

28. What famous collection of pro-Constitution articles was co-authored by James Madison?

29. What New Yorker was probably the first president to hire a staff of writers?

30. What wealthy newspaper mogul is usually credited with getting the U.S. into the Spanish-American War?

31. Who, stricken with cancer and bankrupt, wrote Civil War reminiscences for magazines?

32. What president was seen on America's first transcontinental TV broadcast?

33. Who were the guests on the first televised presidential debates?

34. What president was told by a Scottish newspaper editor that half the people of Britain did not know they were at war with America?

35. Who, on August 1, 1959, was broadcast on both radio and TV in Moscow?

36. In what year were party conventions first televised?

37. Who, at the end of his first week in office, initiated his radio "fireside chats"?

38. Whose was the first presidential funeral broadcast on radio?

39. Who, as a vice-presidential candidate under fire, delivered his famous "Checkers" speech on TV?

40. On what cable TV channel did Bill Clinton answer his famous "boxers or briefs" question?

41. Who did newspaper publisher Philip Freneau accuse of trying to make himself king of America?

42. What skeleton in Grover Cleveland's closet did a Buffalo newspaper find in summer 1884?

43. What was Lyndon Johnson doing to his beagles in a notorious 1964 newspaper photo?

44. What cable news network did the Obama administration shut out of press conferences?

45. What First Lady learned from the newspapers, not her husband, that he wasn't running for re-election?

46. What Republican was caught on tape referring to a certain reporter as a "major-league a**hole"?

Meeting the Press (answers)

1. Richard Nixon, whose downfall was, in some sense, the result of media scrutiny.

2. Jimmy Carter.

3. She sat on his clothes on the riverbank and refused to leave until he granted her an interview.

4. *Time.* The last time was when Nixon died in 1994.

5. "The Hundred Days."

6. George W. Bush.

7. Vice President Spiro Agnew.

8. Dwight Eisenhower, on January 19, 1955.

9. Andrew Jackson. Newspapers could be *very* nasty in those days.

10. Westerns. His aides knew Eisenhower was a voracious reader, one well-read in events of the day.

11. World War I. The memo proved that Germany was proposing a German-Mexican alliance against the U.S. Woodrow Wilson hoped the memo would push the U.S. into the war, and it did.

12. John F. Kennedy, who said, "We had to buy that paper or I'd have been licked."

13. Franklin Roosevelt.

14. Harry Truman, the new president after Franklin Roosevelt's death.

15. Warren Harding. His more reserved successor, Coolidge, did not continue the practice.

16. "Dewey Defeats Truman." He didn't, and a smiling Truman was photographed holding the newspaper.

17. Woodrow Wilson. They were held twice weekly in the East Room.

18. Dwight Eisenhower, who was seen as promoting a sort of generic "faith in faith."

19. Harry Truman.

20. Dwight Eisenhower.

21. Ronald Reagan.

22. The words, "I do not choose to run for president in 1928." Coolidge, who was good at keeping secrets from aides, typed out the slips himself.

23. John F. Kennedy. It is now generally agreed that these articles were ghostwritten.

24. Andrew Johnson. He and the cranky Methodist minister were lifelong political enemies.

25. James Madison.

26. Jackie Kennedy.

27. Andrew and Rachel Jackson. Rachel's divorce from her first husband had not been finalized when she and Andrew married.

28. *The Federalist Papers*, some of them written by John Jay and Alexander Hamilton.

29. Martin Van Buren. These were not only speechwriters, but also writers who "planted" pro-Van Buren articles in newspapers and magazines.

30. William Randolph Hearst, who published a letter from the Spanish ambassador calling William McKinley "weak."

31. Ulysses S. Grant.

32. Harry Truman, on September 4, 1951.

33. John F. Kennedy and Richard Nixon.

34. James Madison. The War of 1812 was a minor matter for most British of the time.

35. Richard Nixon, vice president at the time.

36. 1948, the year of Harry Truman versus Thomas Dewey.

37. Franklin Roosevelt.

38. William Howard Taft's, in 1930.

39. Richard Nixon.

40. MTV.

41. George Washington, who referred to Freneau as "that damned rascal."

42. That he fathered an illegitimate child. Cleveland successfully dealt with it by owning up to it.

43. Picking them up by their ears, which (he said) they enjoyed.

44. Fox News.

45. Grace Coolidge. Calvin was good at keeping secrets.

46. George W. Bush, in the 2000 race.

Making Amendments

Wonderful as the U.S. Constitution was and is, the founders weren't foolish enough to think it was *perfect*. So from the beginning it was subject to being amended, keeping up with a changing nation and changing perceptions of right and wrong. Sometimes presidents resisted the changes, and sometimes they pushed hard for them. Anyway, test your knowledge of the constitutional amendments and the presidents associated with them.

1. The first ten amendments, passed under George Washington, were collectively known as what?

2. The Thirteenth Amendment, ending all slavery in the U.S., was ratified under which president?

3. The Twelfth, allowing for electors to vote separately for president and vice president, was passed under what Virginia-born president?

4. The Sixteenth Amendment, passed under William Howard Taft, gave Congress what dreaded power?

5. Prohibition of alcohol, mandated by the Eighteenth Amendment, was passed under which Democrat?

6. The Twenty-second Amendment, limiting presidents to two terms, was passed under what appropriate president?

7. Under what Republican president was the presidential inauguration moved from March to January?

8. The Nineteenth, passed in 1920, extended the vote to what large group of people?

9. The Seventeenth provided for the direct election of what Federal officials?

10. The Fifteenth Amendment, giving the vote to people of any race, was ratified under what military man?

11. The Fourteenth Amendment, ratified under Andrew Johnson, barred what people from public office?

12. Under Franklin Roosevelt, the Twenty-first Amendment repealed what unpopular earlier amendment?

13. During Kennedy's term, the Twenty-third Amendment gave what area the right to vote in presidential elections?

Making Amendments (answers)

1. The Bill of Rights.

2. Andrew Johnson, in 1865.

3. Thomas Jefferson, in 1804.

4. Collecting an income tax.

5. Woodrow Wilson, in 1919.

6. Harry Truman, who succeeded the four-term Franklin Roosevelt. The Congress, tired of the Democratic presidents, saw to it that no one would repeat FDR's four-term record.

7. Herbert Hoover. The Twentieth Amendment also authorized each new Congress to convene in January.

8. Women.

9. Senators. Before this amendment (1913), senators were chosen by state legislature.

10. Ulysses S. Grant, in 1870.

11. All who had actively supported the Confederacy.

12. The Eighteenth—that is, the Twenty-first repealed Prohibition. This was in 1933.

13. Washington, D.C.

Money Matters

According to St. Paul, the love of money is the root of all evil. Most of our presidents weren't lovers of money, and that includes those who had a lot of it. Still, you can't be president without dealing with financial matters. If the dollar is not almighty, it is a huge factor in U.S. political history.

1. The Eisenhower $1 coin featured what famous event on the reverse? (Hint: space)

2. What territory did Spain cede to the U.S. for $5 million? (Hint: beaches)

3. What Spanish territory did James Buchanan wish the U.S. to purchase for $150 million?

4. Who, for his inaugural, bought his wife a strand of pearls and matching bracelets for $530? (Hint: cabin.)

5. What former general's (and ex-president's) memoirs earned his family $450,000?

6. Who got a reward of $50 for helping capture Redhead Finnigan, a noted horse thief in the Dakota Territory?

7. What future president, an engineer, made a fortune of $4 million between 1900 and 1915?

8. What well-liked president slashed disabled veterans' pensions from $40 to $20 a month?

9. What British statesman claimed he lost $75 playing poker with Harry Truman?

10. What father of a future Democratic president gave Richard Nixon $1,000 for his Senate campaign?

11. What widow was granted an annual pension of $3,000 by Congress in 1870?

12. Who submitted to the national treasury a bill of $450,000 for his Revolutionary War expenses?

13. What was the annual salary for the first president?

14. What master showman offered Ulysses Grant $100,000 to display his Civil War memorabilia?

15. In 1909, what coin became the first to display a president's face?

16. What Republican presented the first *trillion*-dollar budget to Congress?

17. For what did Andrew Johnson offer a $100,000 reward in 1865?

18. For what purpose did Congress grant $35,000 to Benjamin Harrison's wife?

19. What artist's famous portrait of Washington is the basis for the picture on the $1 bill?

20. Who, in the 1970s, mandated a wage and price freeze to combat inflation?

21. What world-changing news in October 1957 prompted Dwight Eisenhower to push for more defense spending?

22. Who, a week before his inauguration, saw the presidential salary double, from $100,000 to $200,000?

23. What metropolis, finding itself in financial straits, appealed to Gerald Ford for aid in 1975?

Money Matters (answers)

1. The 1969 moon landing.
2. Florida. Behind this deal was future president Andrew Jackson, who had booted out the Spanish governor of Florida.
3. Cuba. Congress rejected the proposal.
4. Abraham Lincoln. They were purchased at Tiffany's in New York and are now on display at the Smithsonian.
5. Ulysses S. Grant, who died just after his book's completion and never himself benefited from the royalties.
6. Theodore Roosevelt.
7. Herbert Hoover.
8. Franklin Roosevelt.
9. Winston Churchill.
10. Joe Kennedy, father of the man who defeated Nixon for president in 1960.
11. Mary, widow of Abraham Lincoln.
12. George Washington, who had not drawn any pay during the war.
13. $25,000—considered as being for expenses, not actual pay.
14. P. T. Barnum. Although Grant needed the money, he turned the offer down.
15. The Lincoln penny, at the urging of Theodore Roosevelt.
16. Ronald Reagan.
17. The apprehension of Confederate president Jefferson Davis.
18. Renovating the White House.
19. Gilbert Stuart's.
20. Richard Nixon, in 1971.
21. The Russian launching of the Sputnik satellite. There was fear that the Russians were getting ahead in technology.
22. Richard Nixon.
23. New York. Ford at first resisted giving aid, leading to a famous newspaper headline: "Ford to New York: Go to Hell." Eventually the federal government did provide $2.3 billion in short-term loans.

✷　　✷　　✷

Taxation Good and Bad (Mostly Bad)

The Founding Fathers seemed to believe that where taxes were concerned, the less, the better. How could it have been otherwise, considering a huge part of the colonies' beef against Britain was overtaxation? Throughout our history we have had presidents who never met a tax they liked—but also those who fit easily into the "tax and spend" category.

1. What hated tax commenced in 1913, during Woodrow Wilson's presidency?

2. Who referred to Reagan's plan to cut income taxes as "voodoo economics"?

3. What early president published *A Dissertation on the Canon and Feudal Law,* attacking invalid taxation?

4. What wealthy New Yorker promised to use a progressive income tax to narrow the gap between rich and poor?

5. Who, as a member of Virginia's House of Delegates, opposed taxation for the support of churches?

6. What Democratic opponent of George H. W. Bush was labeled the governor of "Taxachusetts"?

7. What associate of Richard Nixon pleaded "no contest" to a charge of tax evasion?

8. What Republican will forever be associated with the words "No new taxes!"?

9. What earlier Republican impressed Ronald Reagan because he had cut taxes four times?

Taxation Good and Bad (Mostly Bad) (answers)

1. The income tax. At the time, the top rate was 7 percent. (My, how times have changed.)
2. George H. W. Bush.
3. John Adams. It was actually published in London, not America.
4. Theodore Roosevelt.
5. James Madison.
6. Michael Dukakis.
7. Vice president Spiro Agnew, who resigned.
8. George H. W. Bush, who broke this rash campaign promise and (in the next election) lived to regret it.
9. Calvin Coolidge.

✳   ✳   ✳

Pardon Me: The Sometimes Merciful Presidents

"Blessed are the merciful" has always played well in politics. While authorities have to hunt down the guilty and punish them, presidents generate a heap of good will when they pardon someone. But some of the presidential pardons below were not always greeted with applause. Read on.

1. What Republican received from his successor a pardon for any crimes "he committed or may have committed"?
2. To which group of people did Gerald Ford offer a pardon if they would commit to two years of public service?
3. For helping in the 1814 Battle of New Orleans, what famous Louisiana pirate was pardoned by President James Monroe?
4. As one of his first acts in office, President Carter pardoned what group of people?
5. In 1869, President Grant pardoned Dr. Samuel Mudd. With what tragedy had Mudd been connected?
6. What group of people got a pardon from Andrew Johnson on May 29, 1865?

7. Warren Harding pardoned what noted Socialist leader, imprisoned by Woodrow Wilson?

8. Oscar Collazo, who was imprisoned for attempting to assassinate Harry Truman in 1950, was freed by what later Democrat?

9. In what controversial army officer's case did Richard Nixon intervene in 1971?

10. What fugitive millionaire did Bill Clinton notoriously pardon just before leaving office?

11. What disgraced former vice president did Andrew Jackson insist be given a government pension? (Hint: a treason trial)

Pardon Me: The Sometimes Merciful Presidents (answers)

1. Richard Nixon, who received his "unconditional" pardon from Gerald Ford.

2. Vietnam draft dodgers. Not many responded to his offer.

3. Jean Lafitte.

4. Draft dodgers.

5. The Lincoln assassination. It was Mudd that set the broken leg of assassin John Wilkes Booth. Mudd spent several years in prison for this.

6. Most (but not all) former Confederates.

7. Eugene Debs, who was more than once the Socialist candidate for president.

8. Jimmy Carter, in 1979. However, note that Collazo served 28 years in prison.

9. Lieutenant William Calley, who was court-martialed and found guilty of premeditated murder for some of his actions in Vietnam. It appeared that Nixon, like many Americans, felt that Calley was made a scapegoat.

10. Marc Rich, whose pardon was one of several very controversial pardons by Clinton.

11. Aaron Burr, vice president under Thomas Jefferson. Burr was acquitted in the trial in which he was accused of trying to form his own country, but he never lived down the negative publicity and was denied his Revolutionary War pension. Jackson remedied that.

✳ ✳ ✳

Westward Ho! Getting More Land

The phrase "Manifest Destiny" has been used (some might say *misused*) to refer to the U.S.'s gradual push westward. The idea is that the tiny little colonies on the Atlantic seaboard were destined by God or Fate (or ambitious politicians) to expand all the way to the Pacific and beyond. Several presidents had a hand in that project.

1. What president approved, but had little to do with, the purchase of Alaska?

2. What huge tract did Thomas Jefferson authorize purchasing from France for $15 million?

3. And what future president was one of the negotiators of that purchase? (Hint: doctrine)

4. Who supported Georgia in its efforts to oust the Cherokees from the land?

5. What president was primarily responsible for the acquisition of Texas?

6. What territory did Spain cede to the U.S. under the 1819 Adams-Onis Treaty?

7. What Pacific territory did Grover Cleveland *not* want the U.S. to have?

8. Who lost his re-election bid mostly because he opposed the annexation of Texas?

9. Who was the first president to witness territory *withdrawing from* the U.S.?

10. Under William McKinley, what lands did the U.S. acquire from Spain?

11. What tiny, but very important, strip of Central American land is connected with Theodore Roosevelt?

12. Who declared in his "Mobile Doctrine" that the U.S. would never again acquire territory by conquest?

13. What boundary was the Aroostook War of 1839 fought over?

14. Under Franklin Pierce, the Gadsden Purchase from Mexico acquired land that is now in what two states?

15. Who, three days before leaving office, signed a congressional resolution for annexing Texas?

16. Who agreed to the Oregon Treaty of 1846, granting the territory that became Washington and Oregon?

17. What president authorized his Secretary of State to try to purchase Cuba from Spain?

18. What Republican approved the acquisition of Hawaii?

19. To what nation did Franklin Pierce offer $50 for a large chunk of its northern territory?

20. What Democrat was the first to try to purchase Alaska from Russia?

21. What post-Civil War president suggested annexing Santo Domingo and making it a home for former slaves?

22. What Pacific island group, famous in World War II, was annexed by Andrew Johnson's Secretary of State William Seward?

23. What Caribbean island group was acquired in Woodrow Wilson's presidency?

Westward Ho! Getting More Land (answers)

1. Andrew Johnson. The purchase from Russia was mostly the work of his Secretary of State, William Seward.
2. The Louisiana Territory.
3. James Monroe.
4. Andrew Jackson.
5. James K. Polk, who made Texas the centerpiece of his campaign in 1844.
6. Florida. James Monroe approved the treaty, which was negotiated by future president John Quincy Adams.
7. Hawaii. Cleveland condemned American participation in booting out Hawaii's native queen.
8. Martin Van Buren.
9. James Buchanan. After the election of his successor, Abraham Lincoln, states began to secede, beginning with South Carolina in December 1860. While Buchanan was still in office, seven states had seceded.
10. Puerto Rico, Guam, and the Philippines, all part of the fallout of the Spanish-American War.
11. The Panama Canal Zone. The canal was one of Roosevelt's pet projects.
12. Woodrow Wilson.
13. Maine and Canada. Martin Van Buren sent General Winfield Scott to arrange a truce.
14. Arizona and New Mexico.
15. John Tyler, who wanted at least some of the credit for acquiring Texas, a task mostly left to his successor, James K. Polk.
16. James K. Polk.
17. Franklin Pierce.
18. William McKinley.
19. Mexico.
20. James Buchanan. Negotiations with Russia broke down, however.

21. Ulysses S. Grant.
22. Midway.
23. The Virgin Islands, purchased from Denmark.

Adding More States

Yes, we started with the magical number of thirteen originals, but we didn't stay that way long. The nation grew by leaps and bounds until we reached the standard fifty. Curiously, some of our lesser known presidents happened to be in office when lots of new states were added.

1. Under which president were three new states (after the original thirteen) admitted to the Union?

2. Though Thomas Jefferson is remembered for the Louisiana Purchase, what was the only state admitted during his presidency?

3. The first state formed from the Louisiana Purchase was admitted during whose term?

4. With the 1820 Missouri Compromise in James Monroe's presidency, which Northern state was admitted as a "balance" to the new slave state of Missouri?

5. What vacation paradise of today became a state when John Tyler was president?

6. Texas became a state during the presidency of which noted expansionist?

7. California became a state during the presidency of what forgotten man?

8. What "breakaway" state was admitted while Lincoln was president?

9. While Grant was presiding over the nation's centennial, what new state was admitted?

10. A record *six* states were admitted during the presidency of what mostly forgotten man?

11. What "frontiersy" state was admitted during the term of "frontiersy" Theodore Roosevelt?

12. Which two new states, admitted in 1912, made William Howard Taft the first president of the forty-eight contiguous states?

13. Who was president when the last two states were admitted?

Adding More States (answers)

1. George Washington, of course. The states were Vermont (1791), Kentucky (1792), and Tennessee (1796). Technically, there were two others added during Washington's presidency: North Carolina (1789) and Rhode Island (1790), both of which had held out for a Bill of Rights before joining the Union.

2. Ohio, in 1803.

3. James Madison's. It was (surprise!) Louisiana, in 1812.

4. Maine, which (oddly enough) had long been a part of Massachusetts.

5. Florida, in 1845.

6. James K. Polk.

7. Millard Fillmore. The year was 1850.

8. West Virginia, formed from the western counties of Virginia, an area that wanted no part of the Confederacy.

9. Colorado, still known as the Centennial State for being admitted in 1876.

10. Benjamin Harrison. The six were North and South Dakota, Montana, Washington, Idaho, and Wyoming.

11. Oklahoma, formerly known as the Indian Territory.

12. Arizona and New Mexico.

13. Dwight Eisenhower. Alaska and Hawaii were admitted in 1959, making Ike the first president of fifty states.

✳ 9 ✳

Events, Earth-Shaking and Trivial

Key Events, For Better or Worse

There never was a "one-event president" (unless it was poor William Henry Harrison, whose one main event was dying so soon). Every presidency has its clusters of events and issues. Still, quite a few presidents' terms of office are remembered for certain events that are forever identified with the man in office, even if he had little or nothing to do with the event. Try to connect each event here with the individual president.

1. Operation Desert Storm
2. The XYZ affair
3. The Mexican War
4. The Cuban missile crisis
5. The stock market crash of 1929
6. The Civil War
7. The Lewis and Clark expedition
8. The beginning of secession
9. The Spanish-American War
10. The Nineteenth Amendment (giving women the right to vote)

11. The Trail of Tears
12. The War of 1812
13. The Compromise of 1850
14. The Whiskey Ring
15. Admission of six new Western states to the Union
16. The Panama Canal
17. Grenada invasion
18. The end of Reconstruction
19. The Missouri Compromise
20. The Pendleton Act
21. Dollar Diplomacy
22. The Kansas-Nebraska Act
23. The moon landing
24. The New Deal
25. Camp David Accords
26. Ending the Korean War
27. The capture and execution of Saddam Hussein
28. The Webster-Ashburton Treaty
29. The beginning of Reconstruction
30. The Interstate Commerce Act
31. Teapot Dome scandal
32. The Marshall Plan
33. The war on poverty
34. The Kellogg-Briand Pact
35. Whip Inflation Now

Key Events, For Better or Worse (answers)

1. George H. W. Bush.
2. John Adams.
3. James K. Polk.
4. John F. Kennedy.
5. Herbert Hoover.
6. Abraham Lincoln. (If you missed this, please don't tell anyone.)
7. Thomas Jefferson.
8. James Buchanan. But note that the secession occurred because Abraham Lincoln had been elected, though it began before he took office.
9. William McKinley.
10. Woodrow Wilson.
11. Andrew Jackson.
12. James Madison
13. Millard Fillmore.
14. Ulysses S. Grant.
15. Benjamin Harrison.
16. Theodore Roosevelt.
17. Ronald Reagan.
18. Rutherford Hayes.
19. James Monroe.
20. Chester Arthur.
21. William Howard Taft.
22. Franklin Pierce.
23. Richard Nixon.
24. Franklin Roosevelt.
25. Jimmy Carter.
26. Dwight Eisenhower.

27. George W. Bush.
28. John Tyler.
29. Andrew Johnson.
30. Grover Cleveland.
31. Warren Harding.
32. Harry Truman.
33. Lyndon Johnson.
34. Calvin Coolidge.
35. Gerald Ford.

✶　✶　✶

U.S. Events: Who Was President When . . .

1. the U.S. celebrated its bicentennial?
2. 241 sleeping Marines were killed in Lebanon?
3. four people were killed at Kent State University in Ohio?
4. rioters protested the nation's first draft law?
5. the Library of Congress was established?
6. Southern states began to secede?
7. riots occurred at the Chicago Democratic convention?
8. the Korean War ended?
9. the Depression began?
10. Prohibition began (over the president's veto)?
11. Prohibition ended?
12. Aaron Burr was tried for treason?
13. Japan opened ports to American traders?
14. Nat Turner led a bloody slave revolt in Virginia?
15. an earthquake leveled two-thirds of San Francisco?
16. the British torched Washington, D.C.?
17. the first adhesive postage stamps were sold?
18. Coxey's Army marched on Washington?

19. the U.S. bought the "large lump of ice," Alaska?
20. the U.S. acquired Florida?
21. Clara Barton established the Red Cross?
22. the Supreme Court ruled in the *Amistad* mutiny case?
23. the Spanish-American War began and ended?
24. the Scopes "Monkey Trial" was held in Tennessee?
25. The U.S. population reached 300 million?
26. Maine passed the first state prohibition of alcohol?
27. Congress created a national election day in November?
28. the federal government shut down for six days?
29. the Emergency Quota Act set limits on immigration?
30. the sale of alcohol was prohibited at U.S. military posts?
31. New York City got electric power?
32. the Indian Territory (later Oklahoma) opened to white settlers?
33. the Supreme Court ordered the breakup of Standard Oil?
34. the A-bomb was dropped on Japan?
35. the U.S. and the Soviet Union signed the Limited Nuclear Test Ban Treaty?
36. problems with OPEC led to long lines at gas stations?
37. troops were sent to overthrow Manuel Noriega of Panama?
38. Custer and his men were killed by the Sioux Indians?
39. General Motors discontinued its Saturn brand.
40. The Erie Canal opened?

U.S. Events: Who Was President When . . . (answers)

1. Gerald Ford.
2. Ronald Reagan.
3. Richard Nixon.
4. Abraham Lincoln.
5. John Adams.
6. James Buchanan.
7. Lyndon Johnson.
8. Dwight Eisenhower.
9. Herbert Hoover.
10. Woodrow Wilson.
11. Franklin Roosevelt.
12. Thomas Jefferson.
13. Franklin Pierce.
14. Andrew Jackson.
15. Theodore Roosevelt.
16. James Madison.
17. James K. Polk.
18. Grover Cleveland.
19. Andrew Johnson.
20. James Monroe.
21. James Garfield.
22. William Henry Harrison.
23. William McKinley.
24. Calvin Coolidge.
25. George W. Bush.
26. Millard Fillmore.
27. John Tyler.
28. Bill Clinton.

29. Warren Harding.
30. Rutherford Hayes.
31. Chester Arthur.
32. Benjamin Harrison.
33. William Howard Taft.
34. Harry Truman.
35. John F. Kennedy.
36. Jimmy Carter.
37. George H. W. Bush.
38. Ulysses S. Grant.
39. Barack Obama.
40. John Quincy Adams.

✻   ✻   ✻

World Events: Who Was President When . . .

1. Saddam Hussein's Iraqi forces occupied Kuwait?
2. Nikita Khrushchev died?
3. the British Parliament voted to abolish the slave trade?
4. Hudson Taylor went as a Christian missionary to China?
5. Alexander Dumas published *The Three Musketeers*?
6. Charles Darwin published *On the Origin of Species*?
7. Gilbert and Sullivan's *The Pirates of Penzance* premiered?
8. painter Pablo Picasso was in his "Blue Period"?
9. Spanish dictator Francisco Franco died?
10. the French Revolution began?
11. King George III of England died?
12. Mexico abolished slavery, which angered American settlers in Texas?
13. compact disc players were introduced?
14. Napoleon invaded Russia?
15. Elizabeth II became queen of England?

16. Charles Dickens completed *David Copperfield*?
17. Winston Churchill left office as British prime minister?
18. German composer Ludwig van Beethoven died?
19. John Paul II became pope?
20. a World Anti-Slavery Convention met in London?
21. the Russian revolution began?
22. Indian leader Mahatma Gandhi was assassinated?
23. F. W. de Klerk and Nelson Mandela won the Nobel Peace Prize?
24. the Lumiere brothers of Paris had the first public showing of motion pictures?
25. Sir Frank Whittle patented the jet engine?
26. the Catholic church held the Vatican II Council?
27. Emperor Maximilian of Mexico was executed?
28. England's Horatio Nelson defeated the French at the Battle of the Nile?
29. Giuseppe Verdi's opera *Aida* premiered?
30. Leo Tolstoy began *War and Peace*?
31. the Beatles released *Sgt. Pepper's Lonely Hearts Club Band*?
32. Emily Brontë published *Wuthering Heights*?
33. Beijing hosted the Summer Olympics?
34. the Eiffel Tower in Paris was completed?
35. Mao Tse-tung co-founded the Chinese Communist party?
36. George V was crowned king of England?
37. the Boxer Rebellion erupted in China?

World Events: Who Was President When . . . (answers)

1. George H. W. Bush.
2. Richard Nixon.
3. Thomas Jefferson.
4. Franklin Pierce.
5. John Tyler.
6. James Buchanan.
7. Rutherford Hayes.
8. Theodore Roosevelt.
9. Gerald Ford.
10. George Washington.
11. James Monroe.
12. Andrew Jackson.
13. Ronald Reagan.
14. James Madison.
15. Harry Truman.
16. Zachary Taylor.
17. Dwight Eisenhower.
18. John Quincy Adams.
19. Jimmy Carter.
20. Martin Van Buren.
21. Woodrow Wilson.
22. Franklin Roosevelt.
23. Bill Clinton.
24. Grover Cleveland.
25. Herbert Hoover.
26. John F. Kennedy.
27. Andrew Johnson.

28. John Adams.
29. Ulysses S. Grant.
30. Abraham Lincoln.
31. Lyndon Johnson.
32. James K. Polk.
33. George W. Bush.
34. Benjamin Harrison.
35. Warren Harding.
36. William Howard Taft.
37. William McKinley.

Foreign Affairs, Mostly Biggies

Name the presidents associated with each of the following.

1. World War I
2. opening the St. Lawrence seaway in cooperation with Canada
3. war with the Barbary pirates
4. invasion of Grenada
5. the Panama Canal constructed
6. the War of 1812 against Great Britain
7. the XYZ Affair with France
8. annexation of Hawaii
9. the Chinese Exclusion Act
10. the Iran hostage crisis
11. Commodore Matthew Perry's mission to Japan
12. Spain ceded Florida to the U.S
13. Pinckney's Treaty establishing the U.S.-Florida border
14. the Mexican War
15. the Communist takeover of South Vietnam

16. the Treaty of Wanghsia, opening Chinese ports to U.S. ships
17. shaking the hand of Fidel Castro
18. building the Berlin Wall
19. the Clayton-Bulwer Treaty with Britain
20. a "journey for peace" to Red China
21. the Good Neighbor Policy with Latin America
22. the Aroostook War over the Maine-Canada border
23. creation of modern Israel
24. sending Marines to the Dominican Republic
25. an American soldier of fortune was made president of Nicaragua

Foreign Affairs, Mostly Biggies (answers)

1. Woodrow Wilson.
2. Dwight Eisenhower.
3. Thomas Jefferson.
4. Ronald Reagan.
5. Theodore Roosevelt.
6. James Madison.
7. John Adams.
8. William McKinley.

9. Chester Arthur.
10. Jimmy Carter.
11. Millard Fillmore.
12. James Monroe.
13. George Washington.
14. James K. Polk.
15. Gerald Ford.
16. John Tyler.
17. Bill Clinton.
18. John F. Kennedy.
19. Zachary Taylor.
20. Richard Nixon.
21. Franklin Roosevelt.
22. Martin Van Buren.
23. Harry Truman.
24. Lyndon Johnson.
25. Franklin Pierce.

✳   ✳   ✳

Bits and Pieces, Connected with . . .

Here's a test: Look at three items—persons, places, events, things, phrases—connected with a particular president, and name him.

1. Rio Earth Summit, Desert Storm, "no new taxes"
2. Billy Beer, invasion of Afghanistan, gas rationing
3. Chief Red Jacket, Farewell Address, Whiskey Rebellion
4. Ken Starr, Whitewater, boxers or briefs?
5. Peggy Eaton, spoils system, second Bank of the United States
6. Aaron Burr, Lewis and Clark, Tripoli

7. Oregon Treaty, new state of Texas, Mexico
8. Nathaniel Hawthorne, Kansas-Nebraska Act, Jefferson Davis
9. Simon Cameron, George McClellan, Fort Sumter
10. Qadhafi of Libya, Iran-Contra scandal, Robert Bork
11. Detroit riots, Gulf of Tonkin, Model Cities
12. Hurricane Katrina, John Bolton, Osama bin Laden
13. annexation of Hawaii, Spanish-American War, John Sherman
14. Missouri Compromise, Era of Good Feelings, John Quincy Adams
15. Black Friday, Credit Mobilier, new state of Colorado
16. Roscoe Conkling, Charles Guiteau, Star Route scandal
17. John J. Pershing, Federal Reserve Act, Prohibition passed
18. WIN, stumbling, presidential pardon of a president
19. Big Stick Diplomacy, Russo-Japanese War, Pure Food and Drug Act
20. G. Gordon Liddy, Saturday Night Massacre, Spiro Agnew
21. Bonus March, stock market crash, Reconstruction Finance Corporation
22. Marilyn Monroe, Montgomery bus boycott, blockade of Cuba
23. "Date nights," Trayvon Martin, death of bin Laden
24. space race, Nikita Khrushchev, Joe McCarthy
25. River and Harbors Act, Louis Comfort Tiffany, Mongrel Tariff
26. the A-bomb, the Marshall Plan, Churchill's Iron Curtain speech
27. Dollar Diplomacy, breakup of Standard Oil, the Mann-Elkins Act
28. Campobello, fireside chats, "packing" the Supreme Court
29. establishing a budget bureau, Teapot Dome, Nan Britton
30. James Blaine, McKinley Tariff Act, Sherman Anti-Trust Act

31. Sam Tilden, end of Reconstruction, "Lemonade Lucy"
32. "ironclad oath," carpetbaggers, impeachment
33. Bleeding Kansas, South Carolina secession, John Breckinridge
34. White House library, Daniel Webster, California statehood
35. "His Accidency," John C. Calhoun, mass cabinet resignation
36. Millard Fillmore, Clayton-Bulwer Treaty, new Department of the Interior
37. Second Seminole War, Panic of 1837, the *Caroline* affair
38. Potomac skinny-dipping, Tariff of Abominations, John C. Calhoun
39. Battle of New Orleans, Oliver Hazard Perry, George Clinton
40. Alien and Sedition Acts, the Quasi-War, "His Rotundity"
41. Pullman Strike, Panic of 1893, new state of Utah

Bits and Pieces, Connected with . . . (answers)
1. George H. W. Bush.
2. Jimmy Carter.
3. George Washington.
4. Bill Clinton.
5. Andrew Jackson.
6. Thomas Jefferson.
7. James K. Polk.

8. Franklin Pierce.

9. Abraham Lincoln.

10. Ronald Reagan.

11. Lyndon Johnson.

12. George W. Bush.

13. William McKinley.

14. James Monroe.

15. Ulysses S. Grant.

16. James Garfield.

17. Woodrow Wilson.

18. Gerald Ford.

19. Theodore Roosevelt.

20. Richard Nixon.

21. Herbert Hoover.

22. John F. Kennedy.

23. Barack Obama.

24. Dwight Eisenhower.

25. Chester Arthur.

26. Harry Truman.

27. William Howard Taft.

28. Franklin Roosevelt.

29. Warren Harding.

30. Benjamin Harrison.

31. Rutherford Hayes.

32. Andrew Johnson.

33. James Buchanan.

34. Millard Fillmore.

35. John Tyler.

36. Zachary Taylor.

37. John Quincy Adams.

38. Martin Van Buren.

39. James Madison.
40. John Adams.
41. Grover Cleveland.

✳ ✳ ✳

Key Events, For Better or Worse (Part 2)

Name the president associated with these key events.

1. the Consumer Product Safety Act
2. the Non-Intercourse Act
3. the *Exxon Valdez* oil spill
4. the Marshall Plan
5. the treason trial of Aaron Burr
6. the $2.3 billion New York City bailout
7. the Iran-Contra scandal
8. the Oregon Treaty with Great Britain
9. the Alien and Sedition Acts
10. beginning of NASA's Project Mercury
11. the Panic of 1819
12. Three Mile Island
13. Credit Mobilier scandal
14. the Good Neighbor Policy
15. death of two cabinet members on board the U.S.S. *Princeton*
16. the Black Hawk War
17. the Homestead Act
18. the Paula Jones lawsuit
19. the Bonus March
20. the Second Seminole War
21. Pinckney's Treaty with Spain
22. Cambodians seizing the U.S. ship *Mayaguez*
23. establishing the Peace Corps
24. No Child Left Behind
25. economic sanctions against South Africa

26. Marines sent to the Dominican Republic
27. whistleblower protection for federal employees
28. beginning of the interstate highway system
29. Pure Food and Drug Act
30. lowering the voting age to eighteen
31. the Federal Reserve system created
32. Dawes Severalty Act, granting full citizenship to Indians
33. deregulation of commercial airlines
34. Hate Crimes Prevention Act
35. explosion of the first H-bomb
36. Medicare and Medicaid
37. Gold Standard Act
38. Senate censure of Joe McCarthy

Key Events, For Better or Worse (Part 2) (answers)

1. Richard Nixon.
2. James Madison.
3. George H. W. Bush.
4. Harry Truman.
5. Thomas Jefferson.
6. Gerald Ford.
7. Ronald Reagan.

8. James K. Polk.
9. John Adams.
10. John F. Kennedy.
11. James Monroe.
12. Jimmy Carter.
13. Ulysses S. Grant.
14. Franklin Roosevelt.
15. John Tyler.
16. Andrew Jackson.
17. Abraham Lincoln.
18. Bill Clinton.
19. Herbert Hoover.
20. Martin Van Buren.
21. George Washington.
22. Gerald Ford.
23. John F. Kennedy.
24. George W. Bush.
25. Ronald Reagan.
26. Lyndon Johnson.
27. George H. W. Bush.
28. Dwight Eisenhower.
29. Theodore Roosevelt.
30. Richard Nixon.
31. Woodrow Wilson.
32. Grover Cleveland.
33. Jimmy Carter.
34. Barack Obama.
35. Harry Truman.
36. Lyndon Johnson.
37. William McKinley.
38. Dwight Eisenhower.

❋   ❋   ❋

✷ 10 ✷

Domestic Tranquility: Home Life

Where We Lived: Presidential Homes

Well, they weren't *born* in the White House. Before and after their Washington stays, the presidents lived in a wide range of homes—from log cabins to plantation manors to apartments to rooms over taverns. Some of these are now open as museums, while others, long gone, may be marked by a bronze plaque.

1. Who lived in (and is buried at) the Hermitage, near Nashville?

2. What Illinois city has the only house Abraham Lincoln ever owned?

3. What president's family's famous "compound" is at Hyannis Port, Massachusetts?

4. What Virginia boy lived for awhile at Ferry Farm?

5. Who designed Poplar Forest, an octagon-shaped retreat for himself near Lynchburg, Virginia?

6. What military man was born at the Virginia estate called Montebello?

7. What Union veteran's family lived at The Point in Ohio?

8. What ambassador in London named his rented house "Little Boston"?

9. Who grew up spending summers in Maine at Walker's Point, a 26-room "cottage"?

10. Who lived at the 2,700-acre Virginia estate called Montpelier?

11. What name from the Robin Hood legends is given to John Tyler's Virginia estate?

12. Who retired to his home named Wheatland, near Lancaster, Pennsylvania?

13. What small Tennessee town has Andrew Johnson's house, grave, and tailor shop?

14. Who worked an unproductive Missouri homestead that he named Hardscrabble?

15. Who faced jungle discomforts living at Camp Gaillard in Panama?

16. Who lived at a lovely Ohio estate named Spiegel Grove?

17. Who lived in D.C. until his death in 1924?

18. Who, as president, lived in a house on Cherry Street in New York?

19. What loving vice-presidential couple lived at Richmond Hill, a Hudson River mansion?

20. What 20th-century president built Warm Springs, in Georgia, as a vacation home?

21. What president's boyhood home, a log cabin, is near Hodgenville, Kentucky?

22. What couple spent a three-month honeymoon at the bride's Williamsburg home, The Six Chimneys?

23. What president's multi-talented wife designed a home, part-Moroccan, part-Indian, on the Stanford University campus?

24. What First Couple retired to Oak Hill in Loudoun County, Virginia?

25. Who lived on a Tennessee cotton plantation named Hunter's Hill?

26. What Virginia-born man lived in an Indiana home called Grouseland?

27. What presidential widow's Tennessee home was untouched during the Civil War?

28. Who lived with his beloved wife "Crete" in an Ohio home named Lawnfield?

29. Who left the White House to live with his young wife at Westland, their home in Princeton, New Jersey?

30. What Ohio couple lived at The Quarry near Cincinnati?

31. Who lived for a time at Prospect, the 20-room home of the president of Princeton?

32. Who, while involved with war relief for Europe during World War I, maintained homes in London and in Palo Alto, California?

33. Who called his new Virginia home "The Hermitage" but later renamed it?

34. Who lived in the Gates mansion, a gingerbread house in Independence, Missouri?

35. What wealthy New Yorker built the estate Sagamore Hill on Long Island?

36. Who named his Maryland retreat "Camp David" after his grandson?

37. The Octagon in D.C. was the temporary home of what early president?

38. What Texas couple lived at The Elms in Washington?

39. What wealthy man donated his summer retreat house to the Shenandoah National Park?

40. Who was married, and vacationed, at Hammersmith Farm in Rhode Island?

41. Whose posh San Clemente home was known as the "California White House" during his presidency?

42. Whose first home with his wife was the Globe Tavern in Springfield, Illinois?

43. Who used the money earned from his autobiography to buy "The Beeches" in Massachusetts?

Where We Lived: Presidential Homes (answers)

1. Andrew Jackson.
2. Springfield.
3. John F. Kennedy's.
4. George Washington.
5. Thomas Jefferson.
6. Zachary Taylor.
7. Benjamin Harrison.
8. John Quincy Adams.
9. George H. W. Bush.
10. James Madison.
11. Sherwood Forest. Tyler liked this name because, since his Whig party had disowned him, he said he felt like a "political outlaw."
12. James Buchanan.
13. Greeneville.
14. Ulysses S. Grant.
15. Dwight and Mamie Eisenhower. Mamie particularly detested the numerous bats.

16. Rutherford Hayes.
17. Woodrow Wilson, the only president to live in D.C. after leaving office. The Georgian Revival house where he lived is now a museum.
18. George Washington. This was, obviously, before the city of Washington was laid out.
19. John and Abigail Adams, at the time when the national capital was New York City.
20. Franklin Roosevelt. It is often called the Little White House.
21. Abraham Lincoln's.
22. George and Martha Washington.
23. Herbert Hoover's wife Lou. As it happened, they moved to Washington just as the lovely house was completed.
24. James and Elizabeth Monroe.
25. Andrew and Rachel Jackson.
26. William Henry Harrison.
27. Sarah, widow of James K. Polk. Though she was adamantly pro-Southern, the Union armies would not harass the widow of a U.S. president.
28. James Garfield.
29. Grover Cleveland, who occasionally lectured at the university.
30. William Howard and Helen Taft.
31. Woodrow Wilson.
32. Herbert and Lou Hoover.
33. Thomas Jefferson, who gave the home the more famous name "Monticello."
34. Harry and Bess Truman.
35. Theodore Roosevelt.
36. Dwight Eisenhower. The home became, of course, the official presidential retreat.
37. James Madison. It was his temporary shelter after the British burned the White House.
38. Lyndon and Lady Bird Johnson.

39. Herbert Hoover.
40. John F. Kennedy.
41. Richard Nixon.
42. Abraham Lincoln.
43. Calvin Coolidge.

The White House: Beautifying, Renovating, Etc.

Like most old homes, the White House has evolved, with the various presidents adding rooms, renovating, refurnishing, equipping it with the newest technologies. No history of the presidents could be complete without a history of what they did to the executive mansion.

1. What horseshoe-loving Republican had a horseshoe pit installed?
2. What macho man hung his big-game hunting trophies in the State Dining Room?
3. What First Lady had her office set up in the *West* Wing?
4. Who were the "Frank" and "Uncle Cleve" married in the White House?
5. What renovating First Lady designed her own White House china?
6. What golf-loving military man had a putting green installed near the rose garden?
7. Who was living in the White House when gas lighting was installed? (Hint: Mexico)
8. What unpopular president of the 1800s got money from his mother-in-law to refurbish the White House?
9. What New Englander was criticized for having a pool table in the White House?
10. What attractive First Lady's portrait (posed with one of her dogs) hangs in the White House's china room?
11. Under whom were the White House stables converted into a four-car garage? (Hint: fat)

12. What Democrat liked helicopter seats so much that he had one made into his Oval Office chair?

13. What stained-glass master did Chester Arthur engage to transform the state rooms?

14. What Democratic First Family's grand piano crashed through a White House floor?

15. What well-known First Lady purchased for the White House a $458 piano and $28 guitar?

16. Whose fancy furniture, purchased in France, was bought by Congress for the White House?

17. What grieving husband ordered the White House hung with black crepe when his beloved wife died?

18. What fussy, dapper president announced, "I will not live in a house like this"?

19. What bookish First Lady insisted that the White House have a bathtub and a cook stove?

20. What young First Lady, adept at floral arranging, loved to have pansies and jonquils around her?

21. Whose extra-large presidential family led to some major renovations in the White House?

22. What luxury-loving First Lady managed to get Congress to grant $475,000 to renovate the White House? (Hint: New York)

23. What First Family moved out in the 1920s while a third floor was added?

24. What wealthy Republican president paid to have the Red Drawing Room restored to its appearance as it was in James Monroe's day?

25. What First Couple returned to a renovated White House, a project that had cost over $5 million?

26. What early president penned this prayer that is inscribed in the State Dining Room: "May none but honest and wise men ever rule under this roof"?

27. What wine-loving president added a wine cellar to the house and brought his own French furniture?

28. What led to the house being painted *white* during Madison's presidency?

29. What New Yorker was criticized for installing a hot-water tank to heat his bath water?

30. What welcome addition was made to the White House bathtub during Fillmore's presidency?

31. What warm addition did Franklin Pierce make to the house?

32. What communications device was installed while Rutherford Hayes was president?

33. The office suite now known as the West Wing was added under what *very* executive president?

34. Who (famously) got stuck in a White House bathtub?

35. What *very* famous room did William Howard Taft add to the White House?

36. What Democrat had a swimming pool installed?

37. A drawing and painting studio was set up on the third floor by whose artsy Southern wife?

38. What young Democrat, strolling through the upgraded White House gardens, stated, "This may go down as the real achievement of this administration"?

39. Who added a famous balcony that is still called by his name?

40. What woodsy type ordered 20 spittoons for the White House when he moved in?

41. What early president threw out the crimson upholstery in the oval drawing room and redid it in blue, creating the Blue Room?

42. Under what 20th-century Democrat did the White House get an electric dishwasher and a bomb shelter?

43. What elegant First Couple had all the TVs removed from the White House?

44. What item was laid in the ground on October 13, 1792, with George Washington officiating?

45. What device-obsessed president ordered the privies replaced by more modern "water closets"?

46. What recent Democrat (who was energy-conscious) presided over the installation of solar panels?

47. What famous seven-foot rosewood bed is named for a president who probably never slept in it?

48. Who removed the White House's Tiffany decorations for "moral reasons"?

49. The Fish Room—so called because Franklin Roosevelt kept his tropical fish there—was later used for what important group of people?

The White House: Beautifying, Renovating, Etc. (answers)

1. George H. W. Bush.

2. Theodore Roosevelt, of course.

3. Hillary Clinton. Traditionally, First Ladies' offices were in the *East Wing*, but Mrs. Clinton knew that the West Wing was more the center of power.

4. Grover Cleveland and Frances ("Frank") Folsom, in the first presidential wedding held there.

5. Caroline Harrison, wife of Benjamin. She even hired someone to teach classes in china painting.
6. Dwight Eisenhower.
7. James K. Polk.
8. John Tyler. Congress didn't want to pay for new furnishings.
9. John Quincy Adams. As it happened, it was paid for out of his own pocket, not government funds.
10. Grace Coolidge, wife of Calvin.
11. William Howard Taft.
12. Lyndon Johnson.
13. Louis Comfort Tiffany.
14. The Trumans. This led to some long-needed renovations in the house.
15. Dolley Madison, wife of James.
16. James Monroe, who had been an American diplomat in France.
17. John Tyler, on the death of Letitia.
18. Chester Arthur, who did not like the hodgepodge of furniture and insisted on extensive renovations before he moved in.
19. Abigail, wife of Millard Fillmore. Prior to her having the stove installed, all cooking was done on a fireplace.
20. Frances, the young bride of Grover Cleveland.
21. Benjamin Harrison's. The group included numerous children, grand-children, the First Lady's father, and various other relatives. At the time, the White House had only one bathroom.
22. Edith, wife of Theodore Roosevelt.
23. The Calvin Coolidge family.
24. Herbert Hoover.
25. The Trumans, who moved back in on March 27, 1952. The renovated house had 132 rooms and 20 baths.
26. John Adams. Whether his prayer was answered is open to debate.
27. Thomas Jefferson.
28. A fire. After the British sacked Washington in the War of 1812, architect James Hoban chose to use white paint to cover the house's

blackened exterior. While some historians date the name "White House" from this, other historians say that it was referred to as "the White House" even before the burning.

29. Martin Van Buren.
30. Running water. Prior to that, water had been lugged in in buckets.
31. Central heat, at that time fired by a coal-burning furnace. Earlier residents had complained that the fireplaces were inadequate.
32. The telephone.
33. Theodore Roosevelt.
34. William Howard Taft, over 300 pounds. This resulted in him installing a tub big enough for four normal-sized men.
35. The Oval Office, *the* presidential office, that is.
36. Franklin Roosevelt, originally intended as an exercise-therapy spot for the polio-crippled FDR.
37. Woodrow Wilson's. His first wife, Ellen, donated many of her works to charity.
38. John F. Kennedy.
39. Harry Truman. People still speak of the Truman Balcony.
40. Andrew Jackson.
41. Martin Van Buren.
42. Franklin Roosevelt.
43. The Kennedys. But when young Caroline cried about missing "Lassie," they did bring in one TV. (Try to imagine the White House today with just one TV—or none.)
44. The cornerstone for the executive mansion, in which Washington himself never lived.
45. Thomas Jefferson.
46. Jimmy Carter.
47. The Lincoln bed, purchased by Mary Lincoln for a guest room.
48. Theodore Roosevelt, who was offended that Louis Tiffany was notorious for sleeping with married women.
49. Journalists.

Barks, Purrs, and Such: Presidential Pets and Other Critters

Most of the chief executives, like people in general, had pets. In some cases this was the standard one dog or cat per household, but a few presidents turned their living quarters—yes, that includes the White House—into veritable zoos.

1. Who had dogs that "authored" books?
2. What was the name of the Nixons' cocker spaniel, made famous in a TV speech?
3. What was the name of Franklin Roosevelt's beloved Scottish terrier?
4. Which Republican had Scottish terriers named Barney and Miss Beazley?
5. What sort of creature was Old Whiskers, which frolicked in the Benjamin Harrison White House?
6. Who kept in the White House a mongrel named Yuki, found at a Texas gas station?
7. What was the breed of Bill Clinton's dog Buddy?
8. What sort of creature was John Tyler's pet Johnny Ty?
9. What sort of animal was Royal Gift, given by the king of Spain to George Washington?
10. Old Whitey, belonging to Zachary Taylor, was what?
11. Who caught some flack for picking up his beagles, Him and Her, by their ears?
12. What Virginian had hunting hounds with such names as Mopsey, Sweetlips, Drunkard, Vulcan, and Truelove?
13. What president's active wife was often seen walking through D.C. accompanied by Rob Roy, her white collie?
14. What early president had a pet mockingbird that rode on his shoulder and took food from his lips?
15. Who kept his racing horses in the White House stables but raced them under other people's names?

16. What breed of dog was Warren Harding's beloved Laddie Boy?

17. What kind of reptile pets wandered loose in the Hoover White House?

18. What 20th-century Democrat had a houseful of pets, even though he was allergic to animal fur?

19. Nanko and Nannie, beloved pets of Lincoln's children in the White House, were what sort of animals?

20. What name—as a warning to Congress—did James Garfield give to his dog?

21. What New England Republican would walk around the White House with a cat or raccoon draped around his neck?

22. Bo, the Obama family pet, is what breed of dog?

Barks, Purrs, and Such: Presidential Pets and Other Critters (answers)

1. George and Barbara Bush. Barbara was (we assume) the author of *Millie's Book* and *C. Fred's Story.*

2. Checkers.

3. Fala.

4. George W. Bush.

5. A goat, who would sometimes pull the children in a small buggy. Harrison was once caught chasing the goat down Pennsylvania Avenue.

6. Lyndon Johnson.

288 ✳ THE COMPLETE BOOK OF PRESIDENTIAL TRIVIA

7. A Labrador retriever.
8. A canary, one of many pets the Tylers owned.
9. A jackass, given to Washington to use in breeding mules, something that fascinated him.
10. His favorite horse.
11. Lyndon Johnson. He told the SPCA that he did it "to make them bark."
12. George Washington.
13. Calvin Coolidge's wife Grace.
14. Thomas Jefferson.
15. Andrew Jackson, who felt (wisely) that it would look bad for a sitting president to own horses that people bet (and lost) money on.
16. An airedale. At the White House, Laddie Boy had his own valet and was given a birthday party with a cake made of dog biscuits.
17. Two alligators, pets of Herbert Hoover's son Allan.
18. John F. Kennedy.
19. Goats. Sometimes to the distress of guests, the two goats were *indoor* pets.
20. "Veto." Considering how brief Garfield's administration was, the name turned out to be somewhat ironic.
21. Calvin Coolidge. One of the raccoons was named Rebecca.
22. Portuguese water dog.

✳   ✳   ✳

"I'm Outta Here": Post-Presidential Life

Not every president had a post-presidential life—some were assassinated, some died of natural causes while in office. On the other hand, some enjoyed a lazy retirement, while others went on to shine in roles that put their presidencies in the shade.

1. Who, in 1997 at age 72, parachuted from a plane?
2. Who (as if you couldn't guess) retired to his estate, Mount Vernon?
3. What unsuccessful president enjoyed the longest post-presidency life, 31 years? (Hint: the Depression)

4. Who, after retiring to Bel Air, California, was found to have Alzheimer's disease?

5. Whose busy post-presidential life included safaris, writing, and an assassination attempt?

6. Whose pet project in his retirement was the new University of Virginia?

7. Who retired to his lovely Tennessee plantation, the Hermitage?

8. What retired president is associated with Habitat for Humanity?

9. What New Englander wrote his autobiography and the column "Thinking Things Over" for *McClure's* magazine?

10. What unsuccessful president had an admirable tenure as chief justice of the United States?

11. What Republican associated himself with Norman Lear's group People for the American Way?

12. Who enriched his retirement years by marrying a woman 25 years younger?

13. Who died in Richmond after being elected to the Confederate Congress?

14. Whose first important post-presidential event was receiving a "full, free, and absolute pardon"?

15. What ailing man was the only president to live in D.C. after his retirement?

16. What career military man finally made his first settled home in Gettysburg, Pennsylvania?

17. Who, as head of the Princeton University board of trustees, clashed with Princeton's president, Woodrow Wilson?

18. What Texan interrupted his ranching duties to do a series of TV interviews with Walter Cronkite?

19. What Northerner was criticized for his criticism of the Civil War and Lincoln's policies?

20. What retired Democrat hosted Lyndon Johnson at the signing of the Medicare Act?

21. Who left the White House for a global tour in which he met Queen Victoria and Pope Leo XIII?

22. What European leader did retired president Herbert Hoover meet in 1938 and describe as "partly insane"?

23. Who spent his 20 months of post-presidential life as a New York lawyer?

24. Who, en route home after leaving the White House, was in a train wreck?

25. What Tennessean was welcomed back by the hometown that had called him a traitor?

26. Who retired to Oak Hill, with its house designed by Thomas Jefferson?

27. What Southerner had, at only 3 months, the shortest presidential retirement?

28. What New Yorker spent part of his retirement helping form the Free Soil Party and running as its presidential candidate?

29. What unpopular president had a long and glorious career as "Old Man Eloquent" in the House?

30. What two former presidents made an appearance together at Britain's House of Commons in 1855?

31. What Virginian helped establish the American Colonization Society for settling freed blacks in Africa?

32. Who divided his time between his ranch in Crawford, Texas, and a home in Preston Hollow in Dallas?

33. What plantation owner undertook a long, productive correspondence with a former political enemy (and former president)?

"I'm Outta Here": Post-Presidential Life (answers)

1. George H. W. Bush. His one previous parachute jump was from his bullet-ridden plane in World War II.
2. George Washington, of course.
3. Herbert Hoover. He left office in March 1933 and died in October 1964.
4. Ronald Reagan.
5. Theodore Roosevelt.
6. Thomas Jefferson.
7. Andrew Jackson.
8. Jimmy Carter.
9. Calvin Coolidge.
10. William Howard Taft, Chief Justice 1921-30.
11. Gerald Ford.
12. Benjamin Harrison.
13. John Tyler.
14. Richard Nixon, pardoned by his successor, Gerald Ford.
15. Woodrow Wilson. He lived not quite three years after that.
16. Dwight Eisenhower.
17. Grover Cleveland, in a curious clash of a former president and future president locking horns.
18. Lyndon Johnson.
19. Franklin Pierce.
20. Harry Truman.
21. Ulysses S. Grant.
22. Adolf Hitler.
23. Chester Arthur.
24. Rutherford Hayes. The wreck killed two people and injured 20, though Hayes was not injured.
25. Andrew Johnson. Because he opposed Tennessee's secession, his hometown of Greeneville branded him a traitor but later forgave him.

26. James Monroe.
27. James K. Polk, who died in June 1849.
28. Martin Van Buren.
29. John Quincy Adams.
30. Martin Van Buren and Millard Fillmore.
31. James Madison.
32. George W. Bush.
33. Thomas Jefferson, who exchanged numerous letters with John Adams.

✳ 11 ✳

Remembering the Presidents

Monuments, Memorials, and So Forth

There's that hulking Mount Rushmore, that sky-high Washington Monument, and so many others, some stunning, some a bit gaudy, but they all testify to the respect we Americans pay to the men we call "Mr. President."

1. Which four presidents' faces are carved on Mount Rushmore?

2. Quincy, Massachusetts, has a monument to which father-son duo?

3. Whose mother's house is a historic site in Fredericksburg, Virginia?

4. Whose official presidential library is in Atlanta?

5. What D.C. landmark is 555 feet high and surrounded by fifty American flags?

6. Staunton, Virginia, maintains whose birthplace as a museum? (Hint: World War I)

7. A wax museum with figures of presidents and First Ladies is near what famous Pennsylvania battlefield?

8. Grand Rapids, Michigan, has a museum devoted to which Republican president?

9. Whose birthplace is a national monument on the south side of the Potomac River in Virginia?

10. What president's statue is on the capitol grounds in Lincoln, Nebraska?

11. Where would you find a wax museum called the Parade of Presidents? (Hint: mountain)

12. In Disney World's robotic Hall of Presidents, which president stands up and makes a speech?

13. If you took a boat tour on the *Potomac Spirit*, what famous presidential home would you see?

14. What Episcopal church in D.C. is known as the "Church of the Presidents"?

15. Washington's Petersen House is the place where which assassinated president died?

16. Columbia, Tennessee, has the home of the president who masterminded the Mexican War. Who?

17. What president can you see perform "live" in Gettysburg, Pennsylvania, each summer?

18. What president of the 1970s has his birthplace site in Omaha, Nebraska?

19. New Orleans' famous city square is named for (and has a statue of) a president important in the city's history. Who?

20. What two noted presidents' homes are near Charlottesville, Virginia?

21. Which Southern state's capitol has its own Washington Monument, with George on horseback?

22. Which D.C. landmark has its walls inscribed with the Gettysburg Address and the Second Inaugural Address?

23. Galena, Illinois, has the home of what Civil War general and (later) president?

24. What president's imposing life-size statue stands under the dome in Virginia's capitol?

25. Which president's D.C. memorial is on the Tidal Basin?

26. What president's home is open as a museum in Indianapolis?

27. The National Cathedral in D.C. has statues of which noted presidents?

28. What First Lady's home in Lexington, Kentucky, is a museum?

29. Fredericksburg, Virginia, has a Masonic Museum devoted to which president?

30. The Little White House in Warm Springs, Georgia, was the vacation home (and death site) of whom?

31. The Ronald Reagan Presidential Library is near what prestigious California university?

32. Who presided at the dedication of the Washington Monument?

Monuments, Memorials, and So Forth (answers)

1. Washington, Jefferson, Theodore Roosevelt, and Lincoln.

2. John Adams and John Quincy Adams. The monument was set up by Congress.

3. George Washington's. It's the Mary Washington House, which George bought for his mother in 1772.

4. Jimmy Carter's.

5. The Washington Monument, of course.

6. Woodrow Wilson. He was born in the house in 1856.

7. Gettysburg.

8. Gerald Ford.

9. George Washington's. The actual house burned long ago.

10. Abraham Lincoln (did anyone miss this?).

11. Near Mount Rushmore in South Dakota. Apparently the museum's owners didn't think the four presidents on Mount Rushmore were enough for the tourists.

12. Abraham Lincoln.

13. George Washington's home, Mount Vernon.

14. St. John's Episcopal Church. Many presidents have attended service there.

15. Abraham Lincoln.

16. James K. Polk.

17. Abraham Lincoln. Actually, it's an actor, performing at "A. Lincoln's Place."

18. Gerald Ford.

19. Andrew Jackson.

20. Thomas Jefferson's (Monticello) and James Monroe's (Ash Lawn).

21. Richmond, Virginia.

22. The Lincoln Memorial.

23. Ulysses S. Grant.

24. George Washington.

25. Thomas Jefferson's.

26. Benjamin Harrison.

27. Washington and Lincoln.

28. Mary Todd Lincoln.

29. George Washington.

30. Franklin Roosevelt, who died there in 1945.

31. Stanford.

32. Chester Arthur, on February 21, 1885.

Real to Reel: Presidents on Film and Video

American history need not be boring. Just look at *Gone with the Wind*, the most painless way to learn about the Civil War and Reconstruction. Likewise, some fascinating movies have been made about the U.S. presidents. (And, to be truthful, a few snorers have been made, too.)

1. What Republican president was the subject of a controversial 1995 film directed by Oliver Stone?

2. *Jefferson in Paris* (1995) starred what tall blond actor as tall red-haired Thomas Jefferson?

3. In *Forrest Gump*, to what president does Gump show his bare behind?

4. What famous actor (with a famous actress daughter) played *Young Mr. Lincoln* in a 1939 movie?

5. James Whitmore was nominated for an Oscar for his portrayal of a president in *Give 'Em Hell, Harry*. What president was it?

6. *All the President's Men* was concerned with the downfall of what 20th-century president?

7. *Tennessee Johnson* (1943) had Van Heflin playing what unpopular president of the 1860s?

8. What tall, lean actor played Lincoln in *Abe Lincoln in Illinois* (1940)?

9. Alexander Knox played a 20th-century president in what 1944 film? (Hint: World War I)

10. *The Indomitable Teddy Roosevelt* (1983) is narrated by what Oscar-winning actor? (Hint: a general)

11. *JFK*, which focused on the Kennedy assassination, starred who?

12. The Steven Spielberg film *Amistad* featured British actor Anthony Hopkins in the role of which anti-slavery president?

13. The 1973 movie *Executive Action* concerned which assassination?

14. Jane Alexander and Edward Hermann played which Democratic presidential couple in a 1975 TV movie?

15. In the long, long miniseries *Kennedy*, who played JFK?

16. Beau Bridges played Richard Nixon in what 1996 movie?

17. Who played Johnson in the 1988 TV movie *LBJ: The Early Years*?

18. Who did William Devane portray in *The Missiles of October*?

19. The character Jack Stanton in the book and movie *Primary Colors* was based on what Democratic president?

20. Who is the main character in the 1992 movie *Ruby*?

21. What Frank Sinatra movie about a presidential assassination did Lee Harvey Oswald watch just before shooting Kennedy?

22. *Sunrise at Campobello* featured lovely Greer Garson as what unlovely First Lady?

23. What tough-talking president did Gary Sinise portray in an acclaimed 1995 movie?

24. *The War Room* is a documentary about which presidential campaign?

25. What early president did Sam Neill portray in a 2000 TV miniseries? (Hint: a slave mistress)

26. Who played Andrew Jackson in the 1958 movie *The Buccaneer*?

27. In *The Littlest Rebel*, what president does adorable Shirley Temple get to meet?

28. Which president has a small role in *Annie*, based on the comic strip "Little Orphan Annie"?

29. What tall actor, remembered for *The Rocky Horror Picture Show*, played George Washington in a TV mini-series?

30. What queen of TV sitcoms played Mary Lincoln in the TV movie *Gore Vidal's Lincoln*?

31. What tall, lanky actor, best known for his comedies, portrayed George Washington in the 2000 film *The Crossing*?

32. *The President's Lady* had Charlton Heston playing what 19th-century president from Tennessee?

33. What movie about a president has a one-letter title?

Real to Reel: Presidents on Film and Video (answers)

1. Nixon, played by British actor Anthony Hopkins.

2. Nick Nolte. The movie concerned Jefferson's career as American ambassador to France.

3. Lyndon Johnson, in one of the movie's clever mixing of actor Tom Hanks with news footage. The scene was, of course, poking fun of Johnson's displaying his own surgery scar.

4. Henry Fonda.

5. Harry Truman, of course.

6. Richard Nixon.

7. Andrew Johnson, who became president after Lincoln's assassination.

8. Raymond Massey.

9. Woodrow Wilson, in *Wilson.*

10. George C. Scott, who will ever be remembered as *Patton.*

11. Kevin Costner, who, however, did *not* play JFK.

12. John Quincy Adams.
13. John F. Kennedy's.
14. The Roosevelts, in *Eleanor and Franklin.*
15. Martin Sheen.
16. *Kissinger and Nixon.* Ron Silver played Henry Kissinger.
17. Randy Quaid.
18. John F. Kennedy. The 1974 TV movie concerns the Cuban missile crisis.
19. Bill Clinton.
20. Jack Ruby, killer of Kennedy assassin Lee Harvey Oswald. Danny Aiello played Ruby.
21. *Suddenly.* Sinatra forced United Artists to take the thriller out of circulation after learning about the Oswald connection.
22. Eleanor Roosevelt. Ralph Bellamy played FDR. Most people agree that Miss Garson was *much* more photogenic than the real Eleanor.
23. *Truman.*
24. Bill Clinton's, in 1992.
25. Thomas Jefferson. Interesting, since Neill is not an American.
26. Charlton Heston. The title character was pirate Jean Lafitte, played by Yul Brynner (with hair, no less!).
27. Lincoln.
28. Franklin Roosevelt. In the 1982 movie he was portrayed by Edward Hermann.
29. Barry Bostwick. Martha was played by Patty Duke. The two appeared in two separate series, *George Washington,* about his early life, followed by *George Washington: The Forging of a Nation.*
30. Mary Tyler Moore.
31. Jeff Daniels, who has done some Dumb and Dumber movies.
32. Andrew Jackson.
33. W., the 2008 Oliver Stone movie about George W. Bush.

Named in Honor of . . .

This habit of naming things for presidents had a glorious precedent: the nation's capital itself. There has been no let-up in naming (and sometimes *re*naming) things for the presidents. Note in the following questions that some of the less successful chief executives are also honored less.

1. What huggable and ever-popular toy was named for a U.S. president?

2. Washington's National Airport was renamed for what two-term Republican president?

3. Harvard's School of Government is named for what Massachusetts-born president of the 1960s?

4. Harrisonburg, Virginia, has a large state university named for what Virginia-born president?

5. What state has a town that was named for Abraham Lincoln *before* he became president?

6. During the Depression, what presidential nickname was bestowed on shantytowns of unemployed men?

7. What beautiful D.C. building has its three wings named for Presidents Thomas Jefferson, John Adams, and James Madison?

8. What president has the record of having the most towns named for him? (Hint: hickory)

9. Kansas City's sports complex is named for what president?

10. The California gold town of Rough and Ready was named for what U.S. president?

11. A large Chicago park, famous for its enormous Buckingham Fountain, is named for which president?

12. Who is the only president to have a national park named for him?

13. What president was Florida's Cape Canaveral renamed for?

14. The toy logs that have amused generations of American kids are named after what president?

15. Princeton University's School of Public Affairs was named for what president (and also president of the college)?

16. The 88-acre D.C. island in the Potomac River is a park named for which outdoorsy president?

17. The famous Gateway Arch in St. Louis is in a memorial named for which president?

18. What president has a state park named for him near Lancaster, South Carolina?

19. The Library of Congress's concert hall is named for which non-talkative president?

20. What university is only four blocks from the White House?

21. Atlantic Beach, North Carolina, has a conservation area named for which U.S. president?

22. What appropriate name is given to the New Hampshire mountain range that includes Mount Washington, Mount Adams, and Mount Jackson?

23. Where would you find a state park named for Dwight Eisenhower?

24. What Southern state has a capital named for the seventh president, "Old Hickory"?

25. The tallest building in Richmond, Virginia, is named for which Virginia-born president?

26. What ecology-conscious 20th-century president is buried in a bird sanctuary named for him?

27. Which state has a million acres of woodland in the George Washington National Forest?

28. The University of Michigan has its library named for a graduate who became president. Who?

29. After whom is the largest species of American elk named?

30. For whose daughter was the "Baby Ruth" candy bar named?

31. Which president has the most counties named for him, 32 in all?

Named in Honor of . . . (answers)

1. The teddy bear, named for Theodore Roosevelt. He was noted as both a hunter *and* a conservationist, and a cartoon of him sparing a bear cub caught the public's fancy. The cub became the "teddy," and it is hard to imagine childhood without a stuffed bear.

2. Ronald Reagan.

3. John F. Kennedy.

4. James Madison.

5. Illinois. Lincoln christened the town site with watermelon juice. He joked that the town name was a foolish choice, since "no one named Lincoln ever amounted to anything."

6. "Hoovervilles," named after poor President Herbert Hoover.

7. The Library of Congress.

8. Andrew Jackson, who just barely beats out George Washington for the honor. There are not only numerous Jacksons and Jacksonvilles, but even a town named Old Hickory.

9. Missouri-born Harry Truman.

10. Zachary Taylor, nicknamed "Old Rough and Ready."

11. U. S. Grant. The park is (surprise!) Grant Park.

12. Theodore Roosevelt. The park, in North Dakota, is a scenic badlands area containing part of Roosevelt's ranch.

13. John F. Kennedy. Cape Kennedy is site of the Kennedy Space Center. Cape Canaveral reverted to its original name in 1973.

14. Lincoln.
15. Woodrow Wilson.
16. Theodore Roosevelt. The island has a 17-foot bronze statue of TR.
17. Jefferson. It's the Jefferson National Expansion Memorial, named for him because it was Jefferson who made the Louisiana Purchase, opening up the West.
18. Andrew Jackson, who was born in the area.
19. Calvin Coolidge, known as "Silent Cal."
20. George Washington University.
21. Theodore Roosevelt (again), who was an early advocate of environmentalism.
22. The Presidential Range.
23. Kansas, where he grew up. The park is near Emporia.
24. Mississippi. The capital is Jackson.
25. James Monroe.
26. Theodore Roosevelt. It's in Oyster Bay, New York.
27. His home state, Virginia.
28. Gerald R. Ford, who graduated from the school in 1935.
29 Theodore Roosevelt.
30. Grover Cleveland.
31. George Washington.

Grave Matters

America has no royalty, and thus no royal tombs. But we certainly have our well-visited gravesites, those of our chief executives. And some of these are *way* off the beaten path.

1. Who was both born and buried in Hyde Park, New York?
2. Who (as if you couldn't guess) is buried in a brick tomb at Mount Vernon?
3. Whose much-visited grave is in Oak Ridge Cemetery in Springfield, Illinois?

4. Whose tomb in a Massachusetts church has an epitaph beginning, "This house will bear witness to his piety"?

5. Who is buried in Greeneville, Tennessee, the town that also has his tailor shop?

6. What notable accomplishment of Thomas Jefferson is famously *not* listed on his tombstone?

7. Whose grave in Arlington National Cemetery has an "eternal flame" burning on it?

8. What military man's imposing tomb in New York overlooks the Hudson River?

9. Who is buried at his Virginia estate, Montpelier?

10. What former general is buried at Spiegel Grove, his estate near Fremont, Ohio?

11. What Virginian was buried in New York but later reburied in Richmond's Hollywood Cemetery?

12. And what president is buried next to the man in question 11?

13. Who was buried in the Congressional Burial Ground but later reburied at his childhood home near Louisville, Kentucky?

14. What huge man was buried in Arlington National Cemetery, near the grave of Abraham Lincoln's son Robert?

15. What president is buried beside another president, beneath a church?

16. Whose huge tomb in Canton, Ohio, is a national memorial?

17. Who is buried underneath a gazebo at an estate called the Hermitage?

18. What assassinated president is buried at Lake View Cemetery in Cleveland, Ohio?

19. Who is buried in a rosewood casket in Kinderhook, New York?

20. Who is buried in Woodward Cemetery near Lancaster, Pennsylvania?

21. What chunky man is buried in Princeton, New Jersey?

22. What "log cabin" president is buried in North Bend, Ohio?

23. What little-remembered president is buried at Forest Lawn Cemetery in Buffalo, New York?

24. Who is buried in his family plot near Johnson City, Texas?

25. Who is the only president buried in Vermont?

26. Who is buried at the Tennessee State Capitol in Nashville?

27. What one-termer is buried in Concord, New Hampshire?

28. What Republican is buried at Crown Hill Cemetery in Indianapolis?

29. What brassy president was buried at Oyster Bay, New York?

30. Who is buried in a stately tomb in the Washington Episcopal Cathedral?

31. What Ohio-born man is buried in Marion, Ohio?

32. Who is buried in Albany, New York?

33. What Quaker president is buried in West Branch, Iowa?

34. Whose grave is at his presidential library in Missouri?

35. Who is buried in a simple army coffin in Abilene, Kansas?

36. Why is William Howard Taft, who had no military service, buried in Arlington National Cemetery?

37. Whose burial site and presidential museum are in Grand Rapids, Michigan?

38. Ronald Reagan is buried at Simi Valley in what state?

Grave Matters (answers)

1. Franklin D. Roosevelt.
2. George Washington, of course.
3. Abraham Lincoln.
4. John Adams, buried beneath a Congregational church in Quincy, Massachusetts.
5. Andrew Johnson.
6. His two terms as president.
7. John F. Kennedy.
8. Ulysses S. Grant.
9. James Madison.
10. Rutherford Hayes.
11. James Monroe.
12. John Tyler.
13. Zachary Taylor.
14. William Howard Taft.
15. John Quincy Adams, buried in the family tomb with his father, John.
16. William McKinley.
17. Andrew Jackson.
18. James A. Garfield.
19. Martin Van Buren.
20. James Buchanan.
21. Grover Cleveland.
22. William Henry Harrison, who (contrary to his campaign posters) was born in a plantation house, not a log cabin.
23. Millard Fillmore.
24. Lyndon Johnson.
25. Calvin Coolidge, buried with his family in Plymouth, Vermont.
26. James K. Polk.
27. Franklin Pierce.

28. Benjamin Harrison.
29. Theodore Roosevelt.
30. Woodrow Wilson.
31. Warren Harding.
32. Chester A. Arthur.
33. Herbert Hoover.
34. Harry S. Truman, buried in Independence.
35. Dwight Eisenhower.
36. He served as Secretary of War under Theodore Roosevelt. It was Taft's pushy widow, Helen, who pushed for his burial in Arlington.
37. Gerald Ford.
38. California, of course.

Monuments, Memorials, and So Forth (Part 2)

1. Which state maintains its Old State Capitol as a memorial to Abraham Lincoln?
2. California is the only state with two presidential libraries. Which presidents?
3. What 20th-century Democrat's home is the only presidential museum in D.C.?
4. Which state has the Lincoln Boyhood National Memorial? (Hint: *not* Illinois)
5. What president's Ohio home has the gates that were the White House gates during his presidency?
6. In what western state can you see wax figures of all the U.S. presidents?
7. What D.C. church has a chapel of the presidents?
8. Which famed D.C. theatre has been restored to its appearance as it was in the 1860s?

9. The John F. Kennedy Library is in what major city?

10. Who (as if you couldn't guess) was the first president to appear on a postage stamp?

11. Where could you see the Washington family Bible and other memorabilia?

12. The home Poplar Forest, near Lynchburg, Virginia, was whose personal retreat?

13. In what D.C. home did John Adams live after the British torched the White House?

14. What warrior president's statue is in Lafayette Square in D.C.?

15. What U.S. president's statue is found in London's Trafalgar Square? (Hint: early)

16. Which president has a museum dedicated to him in Orange, Virginia?

17. The James Monroe Museum is in which state?

18. What president's Virginia home is on a site selected by another president?

19. Which state's capitol has a huge equestrian statue of Andrew Jackson on its lawn?

20. Where could you see the Lincoln Home National Historic Site?

21. And where could you see the Lincoln Birthplace National Historic Site?

22. Dixon, Illinois, has the boyhood home of what man?

23. A "memorial grove" of pine trees near the Pentagon commemorates what Democrat?

24. The Graff House in Philadelphia commemorates which future president's written contribution?

25. Fort Necessity National Battlefield commemorates a battle in which what future president was a key player?

26. The Jean Lafitte National Historical Park in Louisiana is a memorial to which future president's military prowess?

27. Grant's Farm, where Ulysses S. Grant lived in the 1850s, is near what large Midwestern city?

28. Buffalo, New York, has a bronze plaque as a memorial to whose assassination on the site?

29. The Cincinnati Museum of Fine Arts operates a museum devoted to which famous Cincinnati resident?

30. Campobello International Park in Canada has which Democrat's 34-room summer home?

31. The Eisenhower National Historic Site is near what famous Civil War battlefield?

Monuments, Memorials, and So Forth (Part 2) (answers)

1. Illinois. The Old Capitol in Springfield looks as it did in 1860 when Lincoln was nominated for president.

2. Richard Nixon and Ronald Reagan.

3. Woodrow Wilson's. He lived in the house until his death in 1924.

4. Indiana. It is where Lincoln lived from 1816 to 1830, and has his mother's grave.

5. Rutherford Hayes. The home is in Fremont, Ohio.

6. Colorado, at Colorado Springs's Hall of Presidents.

7. The National Presbyterian Church.

8. Ford's Theatre, site of the Lincoln assassination.

9. Boston.

10. George Washington.

11. The George Washington Masonic National Memorial in Alexandria, Virginia.

12. Thomas Jefferson's.

13. The Octagon, which is now open to the public. It is headquarters for the American Institute of Architects.

14. Andrew Jackson.

15. George Washington. This proves how broad-minded the English are, since Washington, as the leader of the American Revolution, was considered a traitor by the English.

16. James Madison, who was from that area.

17. Virginia. It's in Fredericksburg, and it has some French furniture Monroe bought while he was minister to France.

18. James Monroe's. Ash Lawn is on a site selected by Thomas Jefferson, and Jefferson sent his gardeners to help Monroe plan orchards.

19. Tennessee's.

20. Springfield, Illinois. Purchased by Lincoln in 1844, it is the only home he ever owned.

21. Near Hodgenville, Kentucky. The log cabin at the site is *not* the actual one Lincoln was born in.

22. Ronald Reagan. The house is open to the public.

23. Lyndon Johnson. The Lyndon B. Johnson Memorial Grove was dedicated in 1974.

24. Thomas Jefferson. It was the place where he penned the Declaration of Independence.

25. George Washington, in his days in the French and Indian War.

26. Andrew Jackson, victor over the British in the Battle of New Orleans.

27. St. Louis.

28. William McKinley's.
29. William Howard Taft.
30. Franklin Roosevelt. The park is maintained jointly by the U.S. and Canada and is reached from Maine by the Franklin Roosevelt Memorial Bridge.
31. Gettysburg. The site is where Ike and Mamie lived after retiring from the White House.

Such Intriguing Titles for Books

If you see a book with a title like *John Adams: A Life,* you say, "Aha, a biography of John Adams." Some titles are not so obvious (which is why publishers like to tack on *subtitles* to their intriguing titles). See if you can guess from the titles below which president is the subject of each.

1. *American Sphinx,* by Joseph J. Ellis (hint: a Virginian)
2. *A Puritan in Babylon,* by William Allen White (hint: a *very* quiet man)
3. *A Thousand Days,* by Arthur M. Schlesinger (hint: assassinated)
4. *Before the Trumpet,* by Geoffrey Ward (hint: wealthy)
5. *The President Who Wouldn't Retire,* by Leonard Falkner (hint: a long House career after the presidency)
6. *Mornings on Horseback,* by David McCullough (hint: strenuous living)
7. *The Shadow of Blooming Grove,* by Francis Russell (hint: died in office)
8. *Young Hickory,* by Martha McBride Morrel
9. *Old Tippecanoe,* by Freeman Cleaves
10. *In Pursuit of Reason,* by Nobel E. Cunningham, Jr.
11. *Founding Father,* by Richard Brookhiser
12. *Breach of Faith,* by Theodore White (hint: scandal)

13. *The Fox at Bay*, by James C. Curtis (hint: New York)
14. *An Honest President*, by H. Paul Jeffers
15. *Misunderestimated*, by Bill Sammon
16. *When the Cheering Stopped*, by Gene Smith (hint: wartime, 20th century)
17. *Old Rough and Ready*, by Silas Bent McKinley
18. *Gentleman Boss*, by Thomas Reeves (hint: a New York man)
19. *Flight of the Avenger*, by Joe Hyams (hint: broccoli)
20. *The Hidden-Hand Presidency*, by Fred I. Greenstein (hint: war hero)
21. *Dasher*, by James Wooten (hint: Southern boy)
22. *The Available Man*, by Andrew Sinclair (hint: extramarital flings)
23. *Plain Speaking*, by Merle Miller (hint: 20th-century Democrat)
24. *The Dark Side of Camelot*, by Seymour Hirsch
25. *Many Are the Hearts*, by Richard Goldhurst (hint: a Union general)
26. *One Man Alone*, by Ralph DeToledano (hint: break-in)
27. *Dutch*, by Edmund Morris
28. *A Slobbering Love Affair*, by Bernard Goldberg (hint: recent)
29. *First in His Class*, by David Maraniss (hint: bad boy)
30. *Passionate Sage*, by Joseph J. Ellis (hint: Massachusetts)
31. *The Last of the Cocked Hats*, by Arthur Styron (hint: a Virginian)
32. *The Critical Year*, by Howard Beale (hint: Reconstruction)
33. *Lone Star*, by Robert Dallek (hint: big ears)
34. *Rush to Judgment*, by Mark Lane (hint: assassination)

Such Intriguing Titles for Books (answers)

1. Thomas Jefferson.
2. Calvin Coolidge.
3. John F. Kennedy.
4. Franklin Roosevelt.
5. John Quincy Adams.
6. Theodore Roosevelt.
7. Warren Harding.
8. James K. Polk.
9. William Henry Harrison.
10. Thomas Jefferson.
11. George Washington.
12. Richard Nixon.
13. Martin Van Buren.
14. Grover Cleveland.
15. George W. Bush.
16. Woodrow Wilson.
17. Zachary Taylor.
18. Chester A. Arthur.
19. George H. W. Bush.
20. Dwight Eisenhower.

21. Jimmy Carter.
22. Warren Harding.
23. Harry S. Truman.
24. John F. Kennedy.
25. Ulysses S. Grant.
26. Richard Nixon.
27. Ronald Reagan.
28. Barack Obama.
29. Bill Clinton.
30. John Adams.
31. James Monroe.
32. Andrew Johnson.
33. Lyndon Johnson.
34. John F. Kennedy. Lane's 1966 book was the first (though definitely not the last) to cast doubt on the Warren Commission's conclusion that assassin Lee Harvey Oswald had acted alone.

✹   ✹   ✹

Named in Honor of . . . (Part 2)

1. For whom is Missouri's largest lake named?

2. What private college in Lexington, Virginia, is named for a president?

3. Which Midwestern state capital, named for a president, was founded in 1836?

4. What Virginia fort, noted as Jefferson Davis's prison, was named for a president?

5. Jackson Square is a key tourist draw in what picturesque city?

6. What large Texas city, founded in 1846, was named for a Virginia-born president?

7. What president has a capital of an African nation named for him?

8. Which three state capitals are named for presidents?

9. In which large Chicago park could you see the famous Saint-Gaudens statue of Lincoln?

10. The Alaska mountain Denali was renamed for what president?

11. In what state is Thomas Jefferson University? (Hint: *not* Virginia)

12. What comical "society" meets annually on January 7 to commemorate a little-remembered president?

13. What presidential site is named for Dwight Eisenhower's grandson?

14. The province of Presidente Hayes is in what South American nation?

15. The Center for the Performing Arts in D.C. is named for what Democrat?

16. The Brazilian waterway called the River of Doubt was explored by, and later renamed for, what man?

17. The town of Old Hickory, named in honor of Andrew Jackson's nickname, is in what state?

Named in Honor of . . . (Part 2) (answers)

1. Harry S. Truman. The manmade lake is the Harry S. Truman Reservoir.

2. Washington and Lee University. It was called Washington College

when Robert E. Lee took over as its president following the Civil War.

3. Madison, Wisconsin. James Madison died the year it was founded.

4. Fort Monroe (originally Fortress Monroe), in Hampton, Virginia, completed in 1825.

5. New Orleans. Named for Andrew Jackson, the square is at the center of the French Quarter.

6. Tyler.

7. James Monroe. The nation of Liberia, founded by freed American slaves, named its capital Monrovia. Monroe had supported the plan to set up Liberia.

8. Jackson, Mississippi; Lincoln, Nebraska; and Jefferson City, Missouri.

9. Lincoln Park (duh!).

10. McKinley. In recent years the trend has been to call it Denali instead of Mount McKinley.

11. Pennsylvania.

12. The Millard Fillmore Society. His birthday was January 7.

13. Camp David.

14. Paraguay. The province has this name because Rutherford Hayes helped settle a boundary dispute between Paraguay and Argentina. The province's capital is Villa Hayes.

15. John F. Kennedy.

16. Theodore Roosevelt. (It was called the Roosevelt, not the Teddy.)

17. Tennessee. It is a suburb of Nashville and is not far from Jackson's home, The Hermitage.